Fixed

Coupon Note

High Returns
and Low Risk

Fixed
Coupon Note
High Returns
and Low Risk

Rajiv Aggarwal

 World Scientific

NEW JERSEY · LONDON · SINGAPORE · BEIJING · SHANGHAI · HONG KONG · TAIPEI · CHENNAI · TOKYO

Published by

World Scientific Publishing Co. Pte. Ltd.
5 Toh Tuck Link, Singapore 596224
USA office: 27 Warren Street, Suite 401-402, Hackensack, NJ 07601
UK office: 57 Shelton Street, Covent Garden, London WC2H 9HE

British Library Cataloguing-in-Publication Data
A catalogue record for this book is available from the British Library.

FIXED COUPON NOTE
High Returns and Low Risk

ISBN 978-981-122-503-1 (hardcover)
ISBN 978-981-122-504-8 (ebook for institutions)
ISBN 978-981-122-505-5 (ebook for individuals)

For any available supplementary material, please visit
https://www.worldscientific.com/worldscibooks/10.1142/11958#t=suppl

Desk Editors: Sandhya Venkatesh/Lai Ann

Typeset by Stallion Press
Email: enquiries@stallionpress.com

Printed in Singapore

FOREWORD

The mystery of investing in hybrid instruments is always a great candidate for being unraveled. Private banks have, for the longest while, bundled equity risks in the form of a yield instrument with protection on the downside. However, at various times in the last 15 years, be it the Global Financial Crisis of 2008 or indeed more recently the turmoil of March 2020, these instruments have been vulnerable to the shocks emanating from the volatility. Yet, in these markets, fixed coupon notes (FCNs), as Dr Rajiv has articulated in his book, are a good source for generating yield, particularly when we are witnessing two extreme scenarios:

1. A low interest rate market making the hunt for yield in traditional fixed income almost impossible to achieve. Even United States junk bonds are trading in the two pct region
2. An overheated equity market suggesting that making Alpha is going to be tough in equity markets generally, and dividend investing is out of the window as more and more companies will preserve cash

FCN is an attractive instrument for two very different types of investors: an investor who understands that the returns from equity markets are going to be subdued over the coming years, and an investor who wishes to have an income on a regular basis. This quasi-equity, quasi-fixed income feature makes FCN an instrument which is safer than equity but with returns higher than bonds.

Dr Rajiv's book, at a time like this, comes as a beacon of light as he successfully navigates through the complexities of a FCN instrument in lucid language which will help the average investor not just understand the risks associated with the instrument, but also the strategies to mitigate risk and increase risk return tradeoffs.

Investment is both a science and an art, but very often, even accredited investors are seen making significant decisions based on advice from their bankers or on their own gut feeling. It is important that investors understand the end to end perspective of any investment decision they make, and this book goes a long way in articulating every aspect of investing in FCNs. It surprises me that in spite of FCNs being one of the most popular structured products, at least in Asia, there is no published text on the subject. This book should serve the needs of not only investors, but also young professionals advising such investors.

Dr Rajiv is uniquely placed as a practicing banker to understand all aspects of investing in FCNs and he brings together the years of his experience in an effective and skillful manner. I have no doubt that this book will take you on a captivating journey to understand the mathematics behind investing in FCNs. This understanding will enable you to differentiate between various factors in the decision making process, and will hopefully result in better long-term decision making.

These instruments, though having lower volatility than direct equity, are definitely not invest-and-forget type A systematic tracking of these investments is as important as direct equity. Dr Rajiv brings to life 'what if' scenarios should risk taking go wrong which, as history tells us, often happens. His experience of living through various financial crisis and the tools in the hand of the investor to unwind or liquidate are particularly well articulated. Once an investor understands the science behind these instruments, risk mitigation becomes much easier. The techniques described in the book range from actions which can be taken at the first sign of stress to the actions which come in handy when the investor lands one of the underlying stocks.

Bala Swaminathan
Singapore
September 2020

PREFACE

My experience with Fixed Coupon Notes (FCNs) started soon after I started working in the Wealth Management Industry in 2008. Many Investors had suffered heavy losses on their portfolios. It did not matter whether they were holding Equities, Bonds, or Gold. All asset classes were suffering, albeit to varying degrees. Portfolio diversification was also not able to offer protection. Strong markets during the 2004 to 2007 period had led to an increased Risk appetite, which in turn had prompted some Investors to take leverage against their portfolios. Initial selling in Equities and the resultant fall in the value of leveraged portfolios led to Margin Calls. Inability to arrange additional collateral meant that lenders sold any asset which had a Buyer.

While some of the Investors who had leverage in their portfolio suffered actual realized losses, even the Investors who did not have leverage also saw the values of their portfolios come down. Having cut my teeth in the industry at such a time, I have always been conscious of the Risk in the portfolio of any Investor. One possible way to reduce Risk has been to increase allocation to Bonds rather than Equities. However, this invariably means a lower return as well. While higher returns of Equities remain attractive, not many Investors have the ability to stomach daily volatility of Equity prices. Private Equity offers a respite from daily volatility with perhaps higher returns than listed Equities. However, not everyone has the ability to live with the illiquidity and long gestation period.

This situation made me interested in FCNs as an alternative to both Equities and Bonds. These Structured Products have features of both Equities as well as Bonds. They are like Bonds in the sense that there is a Fixed Income. However, the Principal amount is at risk if the underlyings fall below a pre-determined level. While the basic features of FCNs can be summarized in the two sentences above, there are many nuances which can help in making better investments. Moreover, like any other product, understanding the workings behind the pricing of FCNs can help an Investor achieve his goal. While a majority of Investors see FCNs as a yield enhancement product, FCNs can also be used for creating an Equity portfolio with acceptable cost price. Yield enhancement could also vary from having a high Coupon of say 12% per annum to a low Coupon of 2%, which is more than Bonds of similar rating and tenure.

My experience with FCNs over the past 10 years or so has been quite decent. I cannot claim that all FCNs have returned the Coupons as well as the Principal. Similarly, I cannot claim that I did not suffer Mark to Market losses during the life of an FCN. Many a time I have had to take the delivery of underlying Equities on the maturity of an FCN. However, with experience gained over the years, the proportion of FCNs which resulted in a delivery has gone down. Similarly, the ability to take remedial steps post-delivery has also improved over the years. This experience made me think that if I have had the benefit of a publication on the subject, I wouldn't have had to learn these steps by practical experience. This is what prompted me to write this book. The book is primarily aimed at Investors who are starting to get interested in FCNs. Besides Investors, young Professionals in the Wealth Management Industry should also find it useful as they can learn not only the mathematics behind FCNs, but can also advise their clients better.

In this book, I start by explaining the basic features of FCNs like Coupon, Duration, Issuer, Autocallability, and Currency, and move on to the reasons as to why FCNs are an attractive investment preposition. So Chapter 1 is essentially why should one invest in FCNs and what is an FCN. Knowing the basic features is essential before one can learn the science behind it, and also for creating better products.

Chapter 2 provides the basics of Options, which form the backbone of FCNs. While informed readers may feel like skipping this chapter, I will recommend to read at least the part dealing with Volatility. Differentiation between Historic and Implied Volatility is essential for understanding the science of FCNs.

Constructing an FCN involves several considerations ranging from Stock Selection, Implied Volatility, to Implied Correlation. Of course, we cannot lose sight of the choice of tenure, autocall frequency, Issuer, currency, etc.. While there is no hard and fast rule whether monthly or quarterly autocall is better, knowing the pros and cons of each can help an Investor make the right choice. The next part of Chapter 3 deals with comparing FCNs with the sale of Put Option on individual stocks. Lastly, some simple methods to improve the Strike Price of FCNs are covered in this Chapter.

Next, in Chapter 4, we move on to Performance Monitoring and Evaluation. Though daily variations in the prices of FCNs are much less than Equities, these are still by no means an invest-and-forget type of instrument. Daily tracking of prices helps not only in performance evaluation, but also alert us about the possible need of remedial action. The saying 'a stitch in time saves nine' applies very much to FCNs. A timely action coupled with mental preparedness to let go of gains but not to lose Principal can give superior risk adjusted returns. However, in spite of one's best efforts, there will be instances which result in the delivery of underlyings. Knowing the possible remedies in such situations is equally important.

Chapter 6 is a deeper dive into the mathematics of Options. I have tried to keep it simple and cover the concepts from a practical rather than theoretical point of view. Many a time I have seen interest in knowing as to how Issuers price these products. I have tried to cover these aspects in Chapter 7. Lastly, experience of events of March 2020 is covered in Chapter 8.

On a general note, Investors can choose to skip Chapter 6 and Wealth Management Professionals can choose to skip the first part of Chapter 2. I feel that Investments are both a science and an art. Learning to make better Investments is an ongoing process. This learning is what keeps one motivated.

Rajiv Aggarwal
Singapore
August 24, 2020

ACKNOWLEDGEMENTS

I will like to acknowledge the guidance of Mr Pascal Phou, Mr Siang-Han Chew and Mr Benjamin Dour, who have explained the nuances of FCNs to me over the years. Ms Trina Low has helped with various graphs used in the book. I drew on the experience of Mr Ajay Abrol in learning about the workings of the Issuer. I will also like to express my gratitude to Mr Dominique Jooris for his support and encouragement. Mr Atim Kabra provided valuable guidance regarding the overall project. Thanks are also due to Bloomberg, which is the source of some of the figures. Last but not the least, thanks are also due to Ms Sandhya Venkatesh of World Scientific for her hand-holding for my first publication.

ABOUT THE AUTHOR

Rajiv Aggarwal has been working as a Wealth Manager since 2008. He is currently based in Singapore, one of the major centres for Wealth Management. Prior to this, he has worked in London and Dubai. The examples narrated in this book are his own experiences. He has used his learnings about Fixed Coupon Notes over the years to give practical tips and make readers aware of advantages of the product. Before joining the Wealth Management Industry, he was working for the Income Tax Department in India. Besides holding MBBS and LLB degrees from India, he is a Sloan Fellow from the London Business School.

CONTENTS

Chapter 1

WHAT IS FIXED COUPON NOTE (FCN)

Sam has sold a significant stake in his manufacturing company to a Private Equity Fund for a decent sum of money. While he desires that this pot of money should grow, having seen the effects of the Global Financial Crisis of 2008–09, he finds the equities to be too risky.

He had started the company some twenty years back from a small garage. He built and grew it over the years and was never shy of being involved personally in any of the processes. Being a self-made man, he finds himself to be too much attached to the pot of money he has earned.

He has been reading financial newspapers and finds that the equity markets have gone up by almost four times since their depths in March 2009. He has always loved to buy low and sell high. Now he finds that the S&P 500 index is trading at a Price Earning Ratio of more than 20, as against the past 10-year average of 18. He has read about Robert Shiller's Cyclically Adjusted Price Earnings Ratio (CAPE), which smoothens the earnings over the past 10 years. He feels that currently CAPE is at an all-time (excluding the technology boom of 2001) high of 32, which means that future returns from investing in S&P 500 will not be attractive.

Relationship Managers from Private Banks have been approaching him and showing him track records of their portfolios. He can see that the returns on the typical portfolio consisting of 60% Equities and 40% Bonds were in high teens till 2008. When he asks regarding the future expected returns, most Managers say that Equities are expected to return in mid to high single digits over the next 10 years. He could have thought of investing in Equities if the expected returns were attractive. However, he cannot bring himself to bear the risk of investing in equities if the rewards are not commensurate. He asks his Banker if there is a way to enhance the returns on his portfolio and the Banker suggests that he can increase the allocation to Equities or invest in Private Equity. When Sam digs deeper, he finds that investing in Private Equity means making that part of the portfolio illiquid. Sam has seen a Private Equity Fund pay him way above his expectation for his own company. He is reluctant to entrust his money to someone who was not so commercially savvy while making Sam an offer for his company. Moreover, Sam is already 50 years of age and does not wish to wait till he is 62 before seeing his investment come back.

When he starts to think of investing in Fixed Income like Sovereign Bonds or Corporate Credit, he finds that the expected returns are even lower. Returns on Treasury are sub 2% and the Investment Grade Credit barely increases the returns by 1%. Increasing the tenure of Bonds also does not help. Quantitative Easing by Central Banks has led to a situation where many Bonds are having negative yields. It seems that the whole world is awash with liquidity.

The dilemma he is facing is that he wishes to earn more than what fixed income products are offering and he does not wish to take the risk of investing in Equities at current valuations. There are many of us who face the same dilemma.

Unlike Sam, Kendrick is a young Professional based in Hong Kong. He works for a bulge bracket Investment Bank and has been earning a seven-figure salary for the past few years. His Stock Options have also appreciated in value in the past five years. He feels that money can be made only from Equities and is a perennial Bull. He would love to have a major part of his portfolio in Equities. However, he is not so sure regarding the current geopolitical happenings and also the trade war going on between China and the US. Still he feels that in the medium-term, Chinese Equities will do well. He has identified some specific names but finds them to be trading above their fair value. He thinks that he will buy these stocks if they come down.

His situation has similarities with Sam in the sense that both feel that Equities are overpriced. The difference is that whereas Sam has no long-term love for equities, Kendrick thinks that Equities are a long term buy.

The solution to both the situations is a class of Products called Fixed Coupon Notes (FCN) or Reverse Convertibles. While Reverse Convertible is a more popular name in Europe, FCN is more popular in Asia. However, both are essentially the same product. The name FCN emphasizes two important features of this Product, i.e., this being a Note and the Coupon being Fixed. A 'Note' in investment jargon is nothing but a Bond in which the Investor gives the money to the Issuer and the Issuer makes a promise to pay an interest. The word 'Coupon' refers to the interest that is paid on the amount invested. The word 'Fixed' denotes the fact that the coupon is fixed or guaranteed. However, some variations of the Product allow the Coupon to be paid subject to some conditions.

While 'Fixed Coupon Note' emphasizes the feature relating to payment of interest, 'Reverse Convertible' emphasizes the Risk part of the Product. A Convertible Bond is one where Principal can be converted into Equity at the discretion of the Investor. The Investor will exercise this discretion when the stock is trading above the initially agreed price. The word 'Reverse' denotes that this Product will convert into Equity when the Share price is down, rather than when the stock price is up. In the text hereafter, I will be using FCN.

In view of the current environment of low yields on Fixed Income Products and relatively high valuations of Equities, FCNs have gained in popularity both with Private as well as Institutional Investors. FCN is a popular Wealth Management Product because it gives a guaranteed Coupon, which is higher than the yields on Bonds. There is a saying that there are no Free Lunches in Finance. As the coupons on an FCN are higher than coupons on a comparable Bond, there has to be some Risk associated. The Risk is in the form of an exposure to Equities, albeit at a price lower than current price. Let us say that we do an FCN on the shares of Apple, graphically the Risk Reward can be depicted as Graph 1.1.

As we can see from the Graph 1.1 above, the best-case scenario is that on maturity, the Investor receives his Principal and Coupon. The worst case is that the Investor gets the delivery of shares of Apple at a price of $256 when they are trading below level. The Coupon will be received even in the worst-case scenario.

In the example above, we have seen the outcome when an FCN has a single underlying: shares of Apple. However,

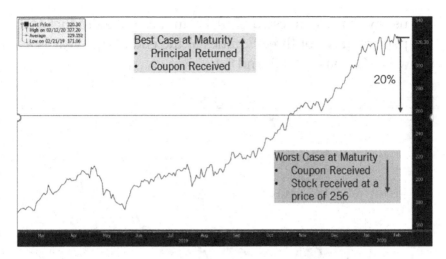

Figure 1.1: Apple Share Price February 2019 to February 2020

usually an FCN has three underlying stocks and in case of fall in price of these stocks, an Investor may end up receiving the delivery of the worst performing stock.

For example, an Investor may invest in an FCN with the following characteristics:

Duration: 1 Year
Coupon: 8% p.a.
Underlying: Apple, Johnson & Johnson, Citigroup (Worst Off)
Strike: 85%

The way it works is that at the end of one year, there is an observation. In case all three Equities close above the level of Strike, the Investor gets his money back with the coupon. However, in case one or more of the underlying Equities close below Strike, we get the delivery of the worst performing stock. The price at which we get the delivery is Strike Price.

Let us say that we invested $250,000 in the above Product and the performances of three Equities at the end of one year is as shown in Graphs 1.2, 1.3, and 1.4.

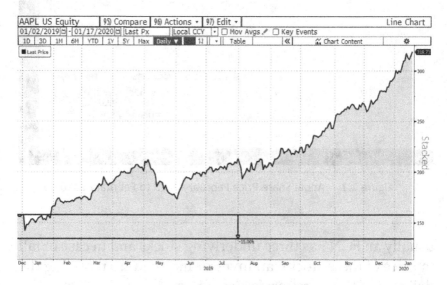

Figure 1.2:   Performance of Apple Shares

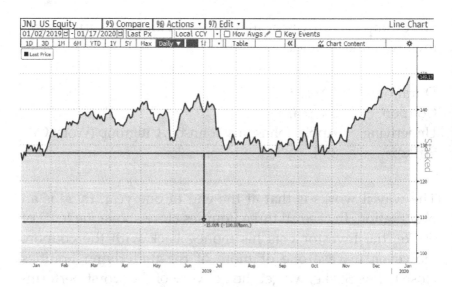

Figure 1.3:   Performance of Johnson & Johnson Shares

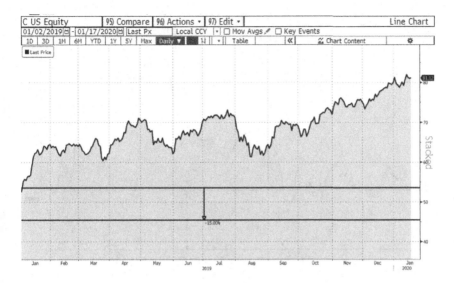

Figure 1.4: Performance of Citigroup Shares

Table 1.1: Performance of Shares Underlying an FCN

Description	Initial Level	Final Level	Percentage Performance
Apple	157.92	318.73	+101%
Johnson & Johnson	127.75	149.17	+16.77%
Citigroup	53.53	81.12	+51.54%

Since in this case the worst performing stock was Johnson & Johnson, which had a positive performance of 16.77%, none of the stocks breached the Strike of 85%. So we will get our Principal of $250,000 and Coupon of 8% ($20,000) back.

Now let us take another example from a different period where the same underlyings closed as per Charts 1.5, 1.6, and 1.7.

Figure 1.5:   Performance of Apple Shares in Example 2

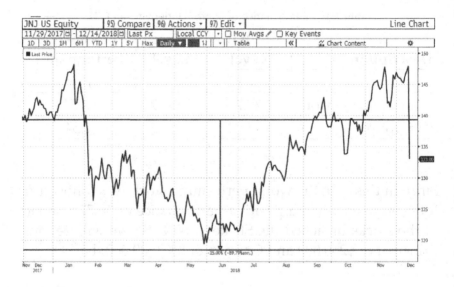

Figure 1.6:   Performance of Johnson & Johnson Shares in Example 2

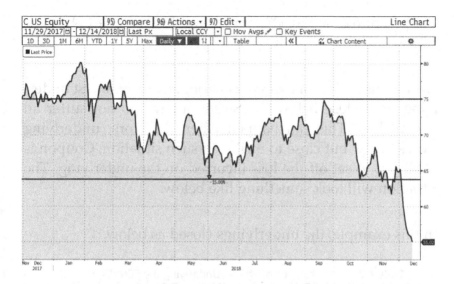

Figure 1.7: Performance of Citigroup Shares in Example 2

Table 1.2: Performance of Shares Underlying the FCN (Example 2)

Description	Initial Level	Final Level	Percentage Performance
Apple	169.48	165.48	–2.36%
Johnson & Johnson	139.33	133.00	–4.54%
Citigroup	75.04	55.02	–26.68%

In this scenario, Citigroup closed at 26.68% below initial level and was the worst performing stock. So our initial amount will get converted into shares of Citigroup at the Strike Price. Let us say we invested $250,000 initially, we will get delivery of shares of Citigroup worth $250,000. Since initial level was $75.04 and the strike was 85% of initial level, delivery will be at a price of $63.78. So we will get 3,919 shares and cash of $46. Since the shares are trading at a price of $55.02, our loss will be 3,919*8.76 = $34,330. Since we would also receive

Coupon at 8% or $20,000, our overall loss will be $14,330 or 5.73%.

Now let us look at one more scenario, where the worst underlying does close below the Strike but we do not suffer an overall loss. This can happen when the worst underlying closes below but close to Strike. In such situation, Coupon is sufficient to set off the loss incurred on the underlying. The situation will look something like below.

In this example, the underlyings closed as below.

Table 1.3:   Performance of Shares Underlying the FCN (Example 3)

Description	Initial Level	Final Level	Percentage Performance
Apple	169	148.72	−12%
Johnson & Johnson	139	118.15	−15%
Citigroup	75	63.00	−16%

Since Citigroup shares were the worst performing, the Investor will get the delivery of these shares. The price per share will be 85% of the Initial Price or $63.75, and the total number of shares received will be 3,921. The value of shares received will be $247,023 which will be lower that the Principal amount invested of $250,000. However, coupon of $20,000 has offset the loss and the net return was 6.81%.

The Product described above is a plain vanilla FCN. However, in practice the most common product has an 'Autocall' feature. This feature means that the product can be autocalled before the expiry of one year. The conditions and the points of time at which it can be autocalled are predefined. Let us say that we have a product which can be autocalled every quarter. The condition under which the Product can be auto-called is the level of the underlying stocks. The most common level is the Initial Price. In this product, at the end of every quarter, there will be an observation. If all three underlying stocks close above the initial level, the product is autocalled. Let us say that the autocall event happens at the end of the first quarter. In this case, we will get the coupon of one quarter or 2% and also our Principal. In case even one of the underlying stocks closes below the autocall level, the product is not autocalled and continues to the next Observation Date. It is immaterial if the worst performing underlying is below Strike on this date. There is no negative consequence and the Product will continue to the next Observation Date.

On the final maturity date, since the product has run its life, the autocall level does not matter. The only thing that matters is whether any of the underlying stocks have closed below the Strike Level. In case any one or more of the underlying stocks have closed below Strike Level, we need to identify the worst performing stock.

DATES

The day we enter the trade is called the 'Initial Date'. Typically, the Bank suggests the Product to the Investor, and upon his agreement the order is placed. This is the day that the 'Risk' of the Product starts. However, this is not the date on which the Investor has to part with money.

The day when the money is to be transferred to the Issuer's account is called the 'Settlement Date'. This is the date from which the reward or the interest on the product starts. Typically, the Settlement Date is two weeks after the Initial

Date. This means that the Investor is carrying the Risk for two weeks more than the period for which it is rewarded.

Once we have settled the Product, the next date is the Observation Date, which can be monthly, quarterly, or semi-annually. Let us say that we have a quarterly observation and the Product is not autocalled, we will get the Coupon for that quarter one week after this Observation Date. Once the Product has continued for its life, the final day is the 'Final Observation Date'. This is the day when the closing prices of the underlyings are observed and number of shares of the worst performing underlying are calculated.

There is one more Settlement Date after this when the Investor gets his money or the shares (in case of underlyings closing below Strike). This is also the date when the Investor gets his Coupon for the period from the last Observation Date to the last Observation Date paid. Typically, this date is one week after the Final Observation Date. Similarly, in case the FCN is autocalled on an intermediate Observation Date, we will get our money back one week after this intermediate Observation Date.

PARTIES

Usually the Investor is dealing through his Wealth Manager who may or may not be the Issuer of the Product. The Product is issued by Investment Banks. Once the Investor and Wealth Manager agree on the specifics of a Product, the Wealth Manager will approach several Investment Banks for a quotation. The trade will be done with the Investment Bank which has provided the best pricing. So the Wealth Manager (on behalf of the Investor) and the Investment Bank (Issuer) are acting as counterparties to each other.

There is a Calculation Agent who is independent of the Issuer and the Wealth Manager. The Calculation Agent's job is to check the levels of underlying stocks on Observation and Maturity Dates. It is the job of the Calculation Agent to calculate the number of shares in case on the maturity date the underlyings close below the Strike Level.

WHY ARE FCNS POPULAR

An Investor is faced with competing choices in terms of asset classes he can invest in. The traditional asset classes have been Equities, Fixed Income, and Cash. Alternative asset classes are Private Equity, Hedge Funds, Properties, and Commodities.

VALUATIONS OF EQUITIES

Following the Global Financial Crisis of 2008, when Investors saw their equity holdings drop significantly, many of them became Risk Averse. Had the valuations of Equities been low,

Figure 1.8: Price Earning Ratio of S&P 500

an average Investor may have gathered the courage to invest in Equities. However, coming to 2020, the Price Earning Ratio of S&P 500 is at 21 as against the average of 18 over the past 10 years.

Even the long-term Price Earning Ratio of S&P 500 is at its highest in the past decade. This index takes the average of real earnings over the past 10 years by taking sector inflation into account. Current stock prices are then divided by these real earnings. This ratio is equivalent to the more popular Cyclically Adjusted Price Earnings Ratio (CAPE) or Shiller Index. The advantage is that this smoothens out the earnings over two business cycles by taking the average of earnings over a 10-year period. This is supposed to be a better indicator of future expected returns. When this index is high, future expected returns are low, and vice versa.

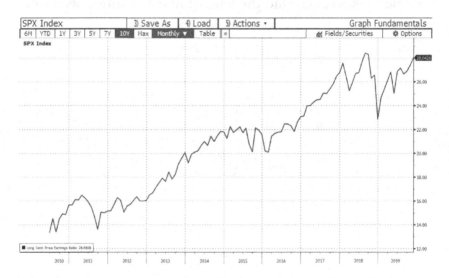

Figure 1.9:   Long Term Price Earning Ratio of S&P 500

At 29.55, it is at its highest level in the past 10 years. In fact, except for the dotcom bubble, it is at its highest ever.

Similarly, Case Shiller Index is at its highest level (except the dotcom bubble) of 32 as against the mean value of 17.

VALUATIONS OF BONDS

Simultaneously, Bond yields are at historically low levels. While further yield compression cannot be ruled out, the scope for such a compression is still quite low. The US 10-Year Treasury is yielding 1.80% as against the lowest levels of 1.50%.

If the yields do not compress further, the maximum you can expect by investing in US Government Bonds is 1.80% p.a.

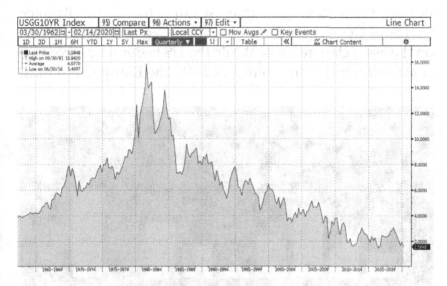

Figure 1.10:   Yield on US Tresury 10 Year Bond

PERFORMANCE OF A 60:40 PORTFOLIO

Traditionally, Wealth Managers have been recommending a diversified portfolio, the most common being comprised of 60% Equities and 40% Bonds. The year-wise performance of this portfolio from 2010 to 2019 is in Figure 1.11.

The average return of their portfolio over the nine-year period was 11.05% and there was only one year with negative performance: 2018. While on one hand, the returns of this portfolio are quite decent, most of it can be attributed to softening of interest rates. When the Fed was raising interest rates in 2018, both Bonds and Equities were losing value. In these circumstances, diversification does not provide that much cushion against the fall in the value of the portfolio.

Besides the softening of interest rates, the size of Balance Sheets of Central Banks is also supposed to have an effect on the asset class returns. While the US Federal Reserve was contracting its Balance Sheet in 2018, the European Central

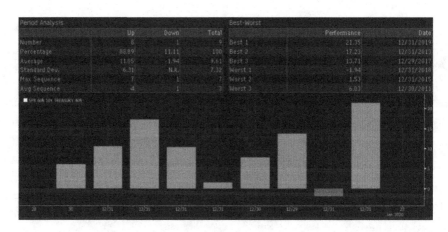

Figure 1.11:   Performance of a 60% Equity, 40% Bond Portfolio

Expansion in central bank balance sheets since the global financial crisis   Graph II.1

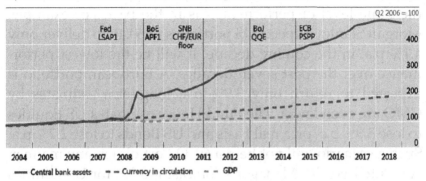

Figure 1.12:   Size of Balance Sheets of Central Banks

This graph aggregates across the six AE central banks that expanded their balance sheets the most over the period (SNB, BoE, BoJ, Fed, ECB and Sveriges Riksbank). Weighted averages of euro area, Japan, Sweden, Switzerland, the United Kingdom and the United States based on GDP and PPP exchange rates.

Bank and Bank of Japan were still in expansion mode. On a global level, the Balance Sheets of Central Banks was still expanding. Simultaneously, only the Federal Reserve was increasing the interest rates while the European Central Bank and Bank of Japan were holding the interest rates. Still, markets could not take the actions of the Federal Reserve in stride and both Equities and Bonds were losing value.

EXPECTED RETURNS

A 60:40 portfolio will not hold in case the three main Central Banks start the normalization of their Balance Sheets simultaneously. While this possibility does not seem likely, any increase in inflation may force the hands of Central Banks. Such an action may affect both Equities and Bonds simultaneously, and Bonds may not be able to provide the protection they are supposed to provide.

Most of the Big Banks do not expect such portfolios to deliver the same level of performance as in the past. For example, Morgan Stanley expects US portfolios of 60:40 to deliver only 4.1% p.a. in the coming decade. It will be the lowest performance over the past seven decades. A European portfolio is expected to return only 3.9% p.a. long-term estimates by GMO are even lower. The Fund House estimates US Equities to lose 3.9% p.a. on a real basis and US Bonds to lose 2.2% p.a. Such a scenario will not help a 60:40 portfolio in any manner. A reputed Wealth Manager's forecast is 5.7% for US Equities and 2.6% p.a. for US Treasuries. So a 60:40 portfolio can be expected to give a return of just 4.5%.

In such a situation, FCNs have provided a relatively safe means of having returns higher than the Bond yields. The logic is that the expected returns from listed Equities are in the range of 6–10%, and in case you invest in Equities, the downside is the same as fall in the price of Equity. In the case of FCNs, since Strike is some 20% below the initial level, the Investor is protected from the fall in the price of the Equity to that extent. Since the Coupon is guaranteed, the actual loss is only when the price of underlying stock falls below the Strike Price by an amount equal to Coupon. In Example 1, if we had invested in the stock of Apple, our losses would be the same as the fall in price of Apple. Whereas in the case of FCN, we do not incur any loss until and unless its price falls by 28% (20%+8%). Another way to look at the situation is that in the worst-case scenario, the Investor gets shares of Apple at a discount of 28% from the initial level.

These features also make FCNs an excellent choice when the economy is in late cycle and the equity markets are toppish. The Investor does not expect Apple shares to go up by 10% in the next one year, so a reward of 8% with downside protection of 20% is specially attractive.

Some other Investors may think that I like Apple shares and would like to own these. However, these seem to be overpriced at the moment and I would prefer to buy these when these have corrected by 20%. In this case, there is a possibility that Investor continues to wait and Apple shares do not come down by 20%. Such an Investor will have an opportunity loss by not earning anything during the wait period. By investing in FCN, the Investor is being rewarded with a Coupon while waiting to get the preferred stock at the desired price.

Of course, there are no free rewards in the financial world. The Investor is giving up the upside in the price of Apple. It is quite possible that the price of Apple may go up by 15% during the life of the product. Besides the upside in the price of the underlying, the Investor is also forgoing the Dividends which would have been received had he purchased the Apple shares on the Initial day.

The Investor is also giving up the liquidity offered by owning the shares directly. Let us assume that instead of directly buying the shares, the Investor has invested in FCN and there is an adverse development. This development could lead to a fall in the price of shares and the Investor wishes to exit his position. If he had the shares with him, he could have sold these on an Exchange. With FCN, the Investor would have to approach the Issuer, who may either give a lower price or may even refuse to buy the FCN. The Investor is also exposed to counterparty risk (more on this later). Imagine someone who had invested in an FCN issued by Lehman Brothers.

FEATURES OF FCNS

There are several features in an FCN which can be chosen to make them suitable for the Risk appetite and reward expectation of an Investor.

INITIAL DATE AND PRICE

This is the date on which the trade is executed and there is no going back. This happens when the other features have been agreed upon between the Wealth Manager and the Investor, and the order is placed with the Issuer of FCN. These features include tenure (six months, one year, or more), Coupon (8%, less, or more), Strike (let us say 80%, the price in percentage terms from the Initial Price), and Autocall frequency (monthly or quarterly).

Having received the order, the Issuer of the Note will go to the market and take an initial exposure to hedge his position. Since the Investor in an FCN is selling a Put Option, and since the Issuer is buying a Put Option, the Issuer has an obligation to deliver the shares of the underlying on maturity at Strike Price. Depending on the mathematical model followed by the Issuer, he will buy certain quantity of shares of the underlyings. Until and unless the Issuer has purchased this initial quantity, he will not issue a confirmation of the trade. The day on which confirmation is issued is the Trade Date.

Since the Issuer is buying the shares of underlying in the market, it is possible for the Investor to specify a price at which the initial trade is done. Let us say that the Investor has agreed on a Strike Price of 80% of the Initial level. This means that while the Strike Price has been agreed in percentage terms, the absolute price is still open. Suppose that Apple shares are trading around $200 but it is possible that by the time the Issuer takes an initial position in the market, share price has moved from $200 to $210. In this case Strike will move from $160 to $168. Maybe the Investor does not wish to take exposure to Apple at a price of $168. In order to avoid such a situation, the Investor is advised to specify the initial level of underlying while placing the order. For example, the Investor can specify that initial price should not be more than $200. This is known as Limit Price.

There are other possibilities as well regarding the initial price. The Investor can specify to do the trade at Market Open, Market Close or even at the average of Market Open and Market Close. Since the initial reference prices of underlyings are determined on the Trade Date, this is also known as Initial Valuation Date.

SETTLEMENT DAY

Though the order has been executed on the Trade Date, no money exchanges hands on this date. The Investor needs to pay the Issuer of the Note only on the Settlement Date. On this date, the cash is paid to the Issuer and the FCN is received. The market practice is to have the Settlement Date two weeks after the Trade Date. This practice is quite different from usual Bond trades where the Settlement takes place two days after the trade. This practice has an important implication for the evaluation of Risk/Reward of a given FCN. As one can imagine, the Coupon will start accruing only when the money is paid to the Issuer. There cannot be any accrual of interest before the money is parted with, so the Reward of the Investor starts from the Settlement Date and not the Trade Date.

On the other hand, the Risk starts as soon as the trade is done. Any adverse price movement before the Settlement Date is to the detriment of the Investor. So as compared to the Reward, the Investor is carrying the Risk for an extra period of two weeks. For a one-year FCN, the reward is for 53 weeks and the Risk is for 55 weeks. For a six-month FCN, the Reward is for 26 weeks and the Risk is for 28 weeks. In terms of proportion, when compared to longer tenure FCNs, the period of Risk is higher in the shorter tenure FCNs. This fact has an important implication for another feature of FCNs: Autocall. Imagine that the Investor has gone in for a six-month FCN with a monthly Autocall feature and the FCN is autocalled at the end of one month. The Investor would have carried the Risk for six weeks and was rewarded for four weeks, an extra 50% of time. However, another way to look at the situation is that since the FCN is autocalled, the Risk of the Investor has ended. A counterargument is that even though the Risk of the existing FCN has ended, now the Investor is faced with the reinvestment risk. In other words, the Investor will have to look for another investment opportunity which may or may not be as attractive. Nevertheless, the savvy Investor should prefer a closer Settlement Date whenever he has a choice.

As the FCN is issued by the Issuer on the Settlement Date, this is also known as the Issue Date.

ISSUER

When an Investor and his Wealth Manager decide on investing in an FCN, the Wealth Manager will go to several Issuers to get a quotation. The bigger Wealth Managers like UBS or Credit Suisse have their own Investment Banks which act as Issuers of FCNs. The other Wealth Managers do not have their own Investment Banks and need to approach third-party

Issuers. Even if the Wealth Manager has his own Investment Bank, the practice is to go to several counterparties. This helps the Wealth Manager in getting the most attractive prices for his client. Unlike listed Equities, where the markets are very liquid and there is a market-determined price, FCNs are customized products and prices given by different Issuers can vary substantially. So getting the quotation from several Issuers is a necessity.

In terms of selection of the Issuer, most Wealth Managers do their own due diligence and will maintain a panel of approved counterparties. When an Investor enters into an FCN trade, he does not wish to have an Issuer which may go bust or may not be able to honor its commitment under the trade. This commitment is akin to the commitment of an Issuer of a Bond who must pay a Coupon and also return the Principal on the maturity of Bond. In any case, FCNs are issued under the Medium-Term Note (MTN) Program of the Issuers. These very programs enable the Issuers to raise debt by issuing Bonds. When an Investor invests in any Bond, the rating of the Issuer is the first thing to be considered. Similarly, selection of counterparties in terms of their creditworthiness is very important. Sometimes, the Investor will opt for a lower Coupon from a better-rated Issuer rather than going for an Issuer whose rating is not that good. So a savvy Investor should always look at the credit rating of the Issuer when deciding on a particular trade.

In terms of seniority of commitment of the Issuer, FCNs are considered as Senior Unsecured liability. This means that FCN liability is ranked below Secured liabilities but above Subordinate Debt. As many of the popular Issuers have also issued Contingent Convertible or CoCo Bonds, FCN liabilities are ranked above these.

The Global Financial Crisis of 2008 had made Investors aware about these issues. However, as time progressed, Investors were paying less attention to the credit quality of the Issuer. The COVID-19 Pandemic has once again brought attention to this.

When an Investor places a cash deposit with a Bank, whether it is in the current account or time deposit, the Bank becomes the Legal owner of this cash. In return, the Bank has an obligation towards the depositor to repay the amount with the agreed interest. So cash deposit enters the Balance Sheet of the Bank as an unsecured obligation. Because it is unsecured, different countries ask their Banks to buy Insurance for these depositors. In case the Bank fails to meet its obligation towards the depositors, the Deposit Insurer is supposed to pay the depositor up to a certain amount. As against cash, the securities placed by an Investor in an account with his Bank technically remains the property of the Investor. The Bank does not become the legal owner of these securities and the securities do not become part of Balance Sheet of the Bank. So when Lehman Brothers went bust, while the Investors who had placed cash deposit lost their money, the Investors who had parked their securities ultimately got their securities back.

The amount invested by an Investor in an FCN is an Unsecured liability of the Issuer. It is on par with the cash deposited with a Bank. In case of bankruptcy of the Issuer, the depositors will be treated as if they have deposited cash. The fact that the Investor is supposed to receive securities under certain circumstances has no bearing. Even if on Maturity of an FCN, the underlyings are trading below Strike Price, the Investor cannot claim these underlyings. His claim will be treated as a claim of cash.

AUTOCALL FREQUENCY AND LEVEL

Once the trade is settled and the Investor has received the FCN in his account, the next important date is the Autocall date. In case of Monthly Autocall, there will be an Observation of the closing prices of all underlyings. In case all underlyings have closed above the Autocall level, the Product will be auto-called. In case even one of the underlyings closes below the Autocall level, the Product will continue to the next Observation Date. The frequency of the Coupon is usually aligned with the Autocall date. Irrespective of the fact that the Product is auto-called or not, the Coupon will be paid by the Issuer.

The frequency of Autocall has an important bearing on the Risk Reward of the FCN. Generally, shorter Autocall frequency increases the chances of the Product being auto-called. From the perspective of the Issuer, they priced the FCN as a one-year Note, but it may get autocalled in one month. So while their payout was for one month, the Investor's Risk was priced for one year. Hence the pricing for monthly autocallable FCNs is usually better (lower Strike or higher Coupon) than the pricing for quarterly autocallable ones.

However, as explained above, the Investor wishes to earn Coupon for a longer duration. It is better for him to go in for longer autocall frequency. In case the FCNs are auto-called frequently, the fee incurred by the Investor can be substantial.

The Autocall level is the price of underlyings at which the Product is autocalled. It is common to have the Autocall level similar to the initial level. However, it is possible to create an

FCN with an Autocall level which is higher or lower than the initial level. A lower Autocall level, say 90% of the Initial Price, increases the chances of the Product being Autocalled. Hence the Issuers will usually offer a better pricing in terms of lower Strike or Higher Coupon. Autocall level need not be fixed. We can have a reducing Autocall level e.g., 97.5% on first Observation, 95% on second Observation, and so on. A reducing Autocall level increases the chances of the Product being autocalled and will usually have a more attractive Strike or Coupon. This reducing Autocall Level also enables an Investor to go in for longer duration FCNs like 3-year or 5-year maturity ones. The longer duration means that the Put Option being sold is more valuable and reducing Autocall level increases the possibility of the Product being called before the Maturity.

FINAL VALUATION DATE

Assuming that the Product is not autocalled on any of the Autocall dates, we would reach the Final Observation Date. The prices of underlyings on the subsequent dates do not matter. There are negative implications for the Investor if any of the underlyings closes below the Strike.

MATURITY DATE

As per market practice, the Maturity Date is one week after the Final Valuation Date. This is the date when the Coupon is paid and Final Settlement takes place.

DENOMINATION

Usually, Issuers insist on a minimum size of $250,000 for the launch of a new FCN. This size enables them to recover their costs in terms of infrastructure used. However, the Issuers allow this investment to be either in a single Note of $250,000 or five Notes of $50,000 each. The lower denomination has the advantage that Investor may choose to square up part of the orginal position after a few months. Same applies in case the Investor wishes to transfer his existing position from one custodian to another.

In the recent years, some Issuers have started allowing for a minimum size of $50,000 for the launch of a new Product. Since they need to recover their cost from a smaller size, naturally the pricing will not be as attractive as the one for a size of $250,000. For an Investor wishing to invest $50,000, the better option is to go in for an already launched product which allows an 'add on' of $50,000. However, one should be mindful of the selection of underlyings. Whether you like the underlyings or not should be the first and foremost consideration before investing.

SETTLEMENT TYPE

When entering into the FCN trade, the Investor has a choice of going in for either a Cash or Physical Settlement. In case all underlyings close above the Strike, the Principal amount will be returned in cash. In case any of the underlyings close below strike, the Principal amount will either be reduced proportionately or be converted into shares of underlying. As an example, if Apple is the worst performing stock and had the following levels:

Initial Level: $300
Strike (80%): $240
Final Level: $200
Amount Invested: $100,000

In the case of Cash Settlement, the Investor will get $100,000 * 200/240 = $83,333.

In the case of Physical Settlement, the Investor's $100,000 will get converted into shares of Apple at a price of $240. So he will get 416 shares, which will be worth $83,200 in today's value. In addition, the Investor will get US$133 in cash.

Though in terms of value there is no difference in Cash or Physical Settlement, there are other implications. In the case of cash settlement, as the price of underlying has been correcting, the Investor is unlikely to venture back by taking a position in the same underlying. A typical Investor would book a loss and move on. In the case of Physical Settlement, the Investor is delivered the shares and tends to hold the shares. If the initial analysis of the Investor about the underlying selection was correct, there is a possibility that the underlying may recover in price. The Investor may go on to recoup the loss or even land with a Profit. This is another attractive feature of FCNs. We know from the insights of Behavioral Finance that most Investors wish to buy when the prices are going up and wish to sell when the prices are going down. By investing in FCNs, an Investor is forced to buy at a lower price, which is good for long-term performance.

Physical Settlement is possible only if the underlying is deliverable. For underlyings like Interest Rates, the physical delivery is not possible. Such Products need to be mandatorily cash settled.

SECONDARY MARKET

Once the Settlement has happened, most of the Issuers will make available a daily pricing of the FCN. Though the

Issuers are under no obligation to do so, daily pricing makes it possible for the Investor to assess his Risk and Performance on an ongoing basis. This pricing is an indicative pricing and in case the Investor wishes to wind up the trade, a specific quotation needs to be obtained. We have seen above that the FCN is basically a sale of a Put Option by the Investor. The price of Put can be affected by factors like Price of underlying, Volatility, Expected Dividend, and Interest Rates. Any reduction in the Price of underlying, increase in Volatility, increase in Expected Dividend, or an increase in Interest Rates can increase the price of a Put Option. The investor has sold a Put option on underlying stock, he wishes the price of option to go down, Any increase in the price of Put option is to his detriment. In such cases, the price of FCN in the secondary market will be adversely affected. In case the underlyings become less liquid, it may become difficult for the Issuer to unwind the positions taken for hedging. This can also affect the pricing of FCN in the secondary market.

Besides the factors affecting the price of a Put Option, there is one more factor which can affect the price of an FCN. Any worsening of Credit Quality of the Issuer means that the credit spread for the Issuer will widen and the prices of Bonds already issued by the Issuer will fall. Since FCN liability of the Issuer is similar to the liability under a Bond, the price of FCN also falls to a commensurate extent.

Investors are well advised to read the Term Sheet issued by the Issuer of the FCN. Some Issuers state that they have hedged the position in the derivative market. In case their counterparty to the derivative trade does not honor its obligation, the Issuer can renege on its obligation. While such conditions do not come under test under normal market conditions, events like the Global Financial Crisis and COVID-19 Pandemic can bring such conditions to the forefront. There are differences among Issuers in terms of the willingness of the Issuers to provide a secondary market price. The market turmoil of March 2020 created a situation where many Investors wished to exit their existing FCNs. While some Issuers think of long-term relations and provide an honest exit price, some others wish to capitalize on the situation and treat the FCN holder as a captive market. These differences in the ethics of Issuers can be learnt by experience. A single Investor may not have sufficient number of investments to see the behavior of different Issuers. However, a Wealth Manager deals with several Issuers on behalf of multiple clients, so a Wealth Manager is better placed to select the right Issuers. A good Wealth Manager will have a panel of about 10 Issuers after considering all these aspects.

LEVERAGE

Most Wealth Managers provide a Lending Value on the FCNs. This Lending Value can be used by the Investor either for maintaining the liquidity or for enhancing the returns. Let us say that an Investor has invested in a one-year FCN and needs liquidity three months down the line. The Coupon is 8% and the Wealth Manager is lending at a rate of 3%. It is possible that one of the underlying stocks has gone down in price and the secondary market price is not attractive. The Investor thinks that by the time FCN matures, this underlying will improve in price. Even if it does not improve in price, the Investor will get the delivery of underlying and he does not mind holding it in his long-term portfolio. In case, he squares up the position, the loss will be booked and there is no scope for recovery of loss. In such situations, the Investor is better off borrowing against the collateral of FCN.

Similarly, leverage can be used to enhance returns. Let us assume that the Wealth Manager is providing a leverage of 50% (or 1:1). The leveraged returns will look as below.

Client Equity:	$100,000
Loan Amount:	$100,000
Total invested in FCN:	$200,000
Coupons Earned at 8%:	$16,000
Interest Paid at 3% on $100,000:	$3,000
Net Gain:	$13,000

So the client stands to earn 13% on the amount invested. The percentage returns will go up as the loan amount goes up or the interest rates go down.

However, we should not lose sight of the increase in Risk. By taking leverage, the Investor is exposed to possible losses on $200,000 worth of FCN rather than $100,000. In case the underlyings close below the Strike, it can result in enhanced capital losses. Even before maturity, leverage can play havoc to an Investor's portfolio. During the March 2020 turmoil, the Implied Volatility shot through the roof and stock prices were falling as if there was no tomorrow. In such situations, the daily Mark-to-Market Price of FCNs goes down drastically. As the prices of FCNs fall, the lending value on the portfolio comes down. On top of that, the Wealth Manager may reduce the Lending Value on different assets including FCNs. This amounts to a double whammy and the Investor will face a Margin Call. In case he cannot come up with additional collateral, the Wealth Manager will liquidate some of the positions in the portfolio. In March 2020, the bid-ask spreads on many Bonds had become very wide. In fact, there were no bidders for many of the Bonds. An

Investor whose portfolio comprised of mainly Bonds and FCNs could not sell Bonds. So the only alternative was to sell FCNs. In the case of FCNs, at least there was a price available. Nevertheless, such Investors had to book significant losses on their portfolios. We cannot blame FCNs for such losses; the blame lies with leverage. If at all, FCNs were relatively better than Bonds because at least an exit was possible. Of course, this experience showed that Equities, though most volatile of asset classes, are at least liquid.

There is another way to look at leverage. Let us assume that the client wishes to earn 8% on his investment. He wishes to earn $8,000 on his investment of $10,000. He invests $200,000 in an FCN with a Coupon of 5.5%. In such a case, he would receive $11,000 as Coupon and pay $3,000 as interest. Still he is left with a gain of $8,000. Now let us compare this with the unleveraged trade in FCN. He has invested in a lower Coupon FCN. Other conditions remaining the same, lower Coupon FCN is safer as the Strike Price will be lower. However, the Investor will be carrying the risk on $200,000 rather than $100,000. Let us say that FCN with a Coupon of 8% has a Strike of 80% and the FCN with a Coupon of 5.5% has a Strike of 70%. In the case of the latter, the Investor is exposed to Risk if the underlying goes below 70% as against 80% in the case of the former. It is a matter of individual preference whether the Investor prefers the former or the latter.

CURRENCY

FCNs can be issued in any tradeable currency. Which currency should be preferred by an Investor depends on several factors. Generally an Investor would prefer his reference currency as the FCN currency. As explained above, the FCNs are issued under the MTN Program of Issuers and there is a Bond component. Naturally, an FCN in a higher yielding currency will have a higher Coupon. So an FCN issued in USDs will have higher Coupon than the one issued in Euros.

Another consideration while deciding the currency of FCN should be the trade currency of underlyings. In case all the underlyings have USD as their trade currency, it is better to have USD as the FCN currency as well. In case all the underlyings are trading in Euro (or any other low yielding currency), having Euro as the FCN currency has the advantage of less complications at the time of Final Settlement. Let us assume that the underlyings are trading in Euro and the FCN is in USD and on maturity, the Investor is to get the delivery of the underlying. In this situation, USDs will be converted to Euros and the Investor will get the shares accordingly. Another possibility is that FCN is in USDs and the three underlyings are in Euro, GBP, and CHF. In case the Investor is to get the delivery, the Calculation Agent will see which is the worst performing stock, convert USDs into the currency of the worst performing stock, and calculate the number of shares to be delivered accordingly. This type of multi-currency structures introduces an element of uncertainty.

Let us say that the underlyings are Roche, Nestle, and Novartis which trade in Swiss Francs (CHF), and Swiss Franc appreciates over the life of the FCN. Appreciation of currency generally has an adverse effect on the share price. So on one hand, share price will drop, and on the other hand, the Calculation Agent will get fewer CHFs against the USDs. This will mean the delivery of fewer shares. The Investor would generally prefer to do such an FCN in CHF. For an Investor with USD as the reference currency, he can either sell USD or buy CHF to do the initial trade or can borrow CHFs against USDs. Borrowing in lower yielding currencies like Euros, CHF, JPY, or GBP is attractive from the point of view of not mixing currency trade with FCN trade. However, when we invest in an FCN in a lower yielding currency, the interest on the Bond component is also low and hence the Coupon is less attractive to that extent.

INITIAL PRICE

While placing the order to invest in an FCN, it is advisable for the Investor to specify the Initial Price of the underlying. Usually to start with, the Investor and the Wealth Manager agree on the terms of an FCN like tenure, Coupon, underlyings, Strike, etc. Strike is defined in terms of percentage of Initial Price. However, the Initial Price is not defined while the rest of the terms are agreed. We will see in Chapter 6 of this book that the Issuer has to hedge himself before issuing the FCN. Since the Issuer may be required to deliver one of the underlyings on the maturity of the Product, the Issuer will buy a small quantity of underlying shares from the market. The Price at which the Issuer buys the initial quantity from the market is known as Initial Price.

It can happen that the Investor and his Wealth Manager have chosen underlyings from markets in different time zones such as Japan, Europe, and the US. It is possible that when the trade is placed, one or more of these markets is closed and the Issuer is not able to buy the initial quantity from the market and would be buying these as and when the respective markets open. In such a situation, the Investor is exposing himself to the risk that the Initial Price may be much above the price at which he is comfortable. In order to reduce this risk, it is advisable that the Investor specifies that he does not wish to enter the trade if the Initial Price of the underlyings is above a certain level. The Investor can choose from Opening Price, Closing Price, Average Price, or Limit Price. This protects the Investor by making sure that the Initial Price and, consequently, the Strike Price are as per expectation. Generally any reputed Issuer will not let its staff members manipulate the Initial Price, still sometimes the Investor feels that the Initial Price mentioned by the Issuer is higher than the price of the underlying. This happens when the stock is not very liquid and the trade size of FCN is large. In such instances, the Issuer needs to spread his buying over a longer period. Specifying a Limit for the Initial Price brings peace of mind to everyone: Investor, Wealth Manager, and the Issuer. The downside is that there is a possibility that the underlying trades above Limit Price and the Investor loses out on trade. Another possible situation is that the Issuer is able to buy only part of the quantity in order to hedge at the specified Limit Price. So it is advisable for the Investor to specify from the beginning whether he will accept part execution.

CORPORATE ACTION

During the life of an FCN, it is possible that an underlying company may have corporate action. Corporate action may range from something simple like change of name of the company to something like liquidation of the company. More common examples of Corporate Action will be stock split, spin off, merger & acquisition, issue of new capital. In such situations, Calculation Agent will determine the change of terms of FCN. If there is a stock split in the ratio of 2:1, the Strike Price, Autocall price and number of shares may have to be adjusted. Calculation Agent will make these adjustments and issue a new Term Sheet to the Investor.

Chapter 2

OPTIONS BASICS

In order to understand Fixed Coupon Notes (FCNs) one must understand the basics of Options. In the financial world, 'Option' is the same as its literal meaning. The Merriam-Webster Dictionary defines Option as 'the power or right to choose'. When one has an Option, it means that he has the right to choose. In the financial parlance, this is usually associated with the right to buy or sell.

Let us assume that you have recently moved to New York to take up a new job. Your real estate agent has shown you an apartment and you really like the apartment. However, at this point in time you are not sure whether this new job will meet your expectations. So you do not wish to commit your savings for buying this apartment. You are thinking that in case this job is as good as you think, you will buy this apartment. You will be sure of your decision only in six months' time. At the same time, you are apprehensive about the price of the apartment going up or the apartment being sold to someone else. So you request the owner to give you six months' time to decide. The owner agrees but demands that you agree on a price and also pay him an upfront amount to secure this right to buy.

In the financial world, this right to buy is known as Call Option. You have the right to purchase the apartment at the agreed price in six months' time. The upfront amount paid by you to secure this right is known as Call Premium. You are the Buyer of this Call and the apartment owner is the Seller of this Call. The price at which you have agreed to buy and the apartment owner has agreed to sell is known as Strike Price.

We can apply the same principle to the shares of Apple. Let us say that Apple is trading at a price of $320 per share. When you buy a Call on the shares of Apple, you have the right to buy these shares. The price at which you have the right to buy the shares of Apple is known as Strike Price. The amount paid by you to secure this right is called Call Premium. As a purchaser of this Call Option you are under no obligation to buy the shares. Unlike the apartment, where there can be other factors besides the prevailing price in six months' time which may influence your decision to buy or not to buy the apartment, in the case of Apple shares, the deciding factor will be whether the shares of Apple are trading above Strike Price. In the case where Apple is trading above Strike Price, you will buy the shares. However, your Profit or Loss can only be determined by including the Premium paid by you in the calculation. Since you have paid the Premium upfront, you are starting with a cash outgo. The final calculation of the trade will be:

Profit or Loss = Market Price – Strike Price – Option Premium.

The Profit and Loss drawn on a graph is shown in Figure 2.1.

So your losses are capped at the Premium paid by you. At the same time, you have the possibility of earning unlimited profits as the shares of Apple go up.

Buyer of a Call Option

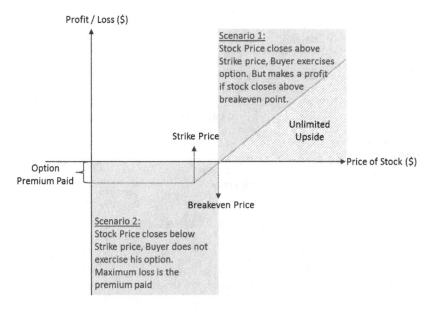

Figure 2.1: The Risk Reward of the Buyer of a Call Option

Now let us look at the above example from the perspective of the apartment owner. Having sold you the option to buy his apartment, he is no longer in control of the decision whether his apartment will be sold or not. At the same time, he has placed himself under an obligation to sell his apartment at the agreed price. He has been compensated for this loss of control over decision making by the Premium paid by you.

Applying the same principle to Apple shares, the seller of the Call Option has lost the control over the decision to sell his Apple shares. That right has been given to you as the purchaser of the Call Option. Should you decide to exercise your right in six months' time, the seller of the Call Option will be under an obligation to sell you the Apple shares at the agreed price. The seller of the Call Option will make profit on the trade only if Apple shares are trading below Strike Price. In

Seller of a Call Option

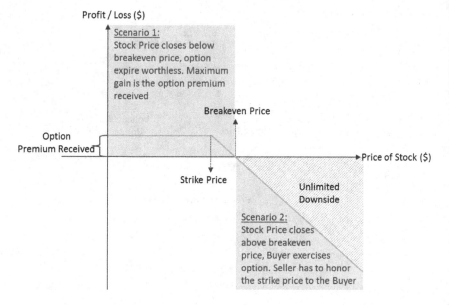

Figure 2.2:   Risk Reward of the Seller of a Call Option

that case he would pocket the Premium paid by you. His position on a graph is as shown in Figure 2.2.

We can see that his upside is capped at the Premium received by him. In case the shares of Apple rally above the Strike Price, he has a loss equivalent to the difference in Market Price and Strike Price. The mathematical formula will look like:

Profit = Max (Premium, (Strike Price – Market Price))

Usually he will try to limit his losses by entering into this trade when he already owns the shares of Apple at the time of selling the Call Option. This is known as Covered Call. In this situation, he is giving up the upside on the shares already owned by him. The owner of the apartment will sell the Call Option only if he already owns the apartment. However, in case of shares of Apple it is possible to sell a Call Option without owning the shares. This is known as Naked Selling. In the situation that the Buyer of Call Option exercises his right to buy the shares, the Seller will have to procure the shares from the market and deliver them to the Buyer. Honoring of the obligation through delivery of shares is known as Physical Settlement. There is another possibility that the Buyer and Seller agree in advance that there will be no exchange of shares and the difference will be settled by payment of cash. This is known as Cash Settled trade. We have seen the advantages and disadvantages of Physical and Cash Settlement in Chapter 1.

Now let us look at another set of transactions. You own an apartment in Singapore and a potential Buyer approaches you to buy your apartment. At that point of time you are not sure whether you are moving to another country. You will come to know about this opportunity in another country in six months' time. This potential Buyer is offering you a good price and you are apprehensive that you may not get the same price in six months' time. So you ask this potential Buyer for six months to decide. Since this Buyer also wishes to lock in the deal, he gives you an option to sell him your apartment in six months' time. Both of you will also need to agree on the price of the apartment.

In this example the potential Buyer has sold you an option that in six months' time, you can choose to sell your apartment to him. However, you are under no obligation to sell your apartment. Rather this potential Buyer is under an obligation to buy the apartment at the agreed price, should you decide to sell the apartment. So you are the owner of this option and the potential Buyer has sold you this option. In the financial world, this option which gives somebody a right to sell is called Put Option.

Applying the same principles to Apple shares, you are the owner of Apple Shares. You are concerned that these shares may fall in value in six months' time. Yet you do not wish to sell these shares today as the shares may appreciate in value. So what you do is to buy a Put Option on Apple shares. Let us say that these shares are trading at $320 per share. You may buy the Put Option to sell these shares at a price of $310 in six months' time.

Your Profit or Loss on this trade in six months' time will depend on the prevailing price of Apple shares at that point of time. You will earn a profit if the Premium paid by you is less than the erosion in the price of Apple shares. In case Apple shares have appreciated in value, you would simply lose the Premium. In a way, you can consider this trade as having bought an Insurance, so that you protect yourself against the fall in the price of Apple shares. Mathematically, your Profit and Loss can be represented as below.

Profit or Loss = Premium Paid – (Final Price – Initial Price)

Maximum loss is capped at the amount of Premium paid. Graphically, the payoff can be represented as below.

Now let us look at the same transaction from the perspective of your counterparty. This person has sold you an option to sell Apple shares in six months' time at a price of $320. He has

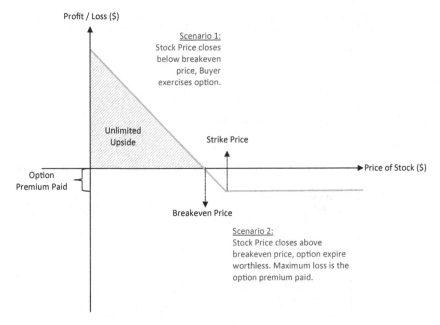

Figure 2.3: Risk Reward of the Buyer of a Put Option

received the Premium upfront. His Profit is maximum when the price of Apple shares does not fall and you do not exercise your right. In this case he simply pockets the Premium. Graphically, his payoff can be represented as below.

The situation of the Put Option Seller can be compared to an Insurance company selling you an Insurance linked to the occurrence of a particular event. The Insurance company would receive the Premium upfront and makes a profit if the insured event does not take place. You may wonder how come Insurance Companies are able to maintain their profitability even though Insured events keep on happening. The reason is that the Insurance companies have statistical models to predict the frequency of such events. They will profit as long as the frequency of actual occurrence of Insured events remains lower than the frequency forecasted by their models.

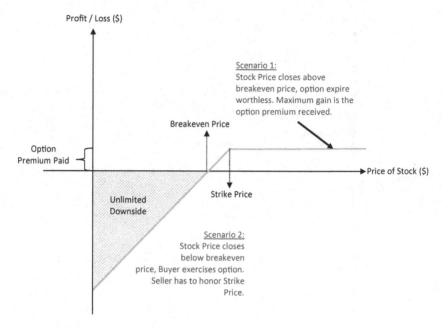

Figure 2.4:   Risk Reward of a Seller of a Put Option (Investor in FCN)

Simplistically, the Buyer of a Put Option is buying an Insurance against the fall in value of something. The Seller of a Put Option, on the other hand, is interested in earning a Premium. Similarly, the buyer of a Call Option wishes to benefit from the rise in value of an asset. The Seller of a Call Option is interested in earning a Premium. In the case of a Seller of a Covered Call, he may forgo the appreciation in the value of shares beyond a certain price. Similarly, a seller of a Put Option may not just be selling an Insurance, and may actually be interested in buying the asset at a lower price.

This price known as Strike Price need not be the same as current market price. You may be ready to absorb a bit of loss in value. So instead of a Strike Price of $320, you may go in for the price of $288, which is 10% below the current price. Of course, you will need to shell out some Premium upfront. When the

Strike Price is the same as current market price, it is known as 'at the money' option. When the Strike Price is below the current market price, it is known as 'out of the money' option.

WHERE ARE OPTIONS TRADED

Broadly there are two Platforms for trading options: Exchanges and OTC. The Chicago Mercantile Exchange is the biggest Exchange where trading on Equity Options takes place. Each Exchange will have specific contracts with different underlyings, maturity, Strike, nature (Call or Put), contract size (in term of number of shares), etc. There are predefined rules whether on maturity, each contract will be settled by way of delivery of underlying or exchange of cash. Prices at which these contracts trade are disclosed, and a typical page on Bloomberg will look as below.

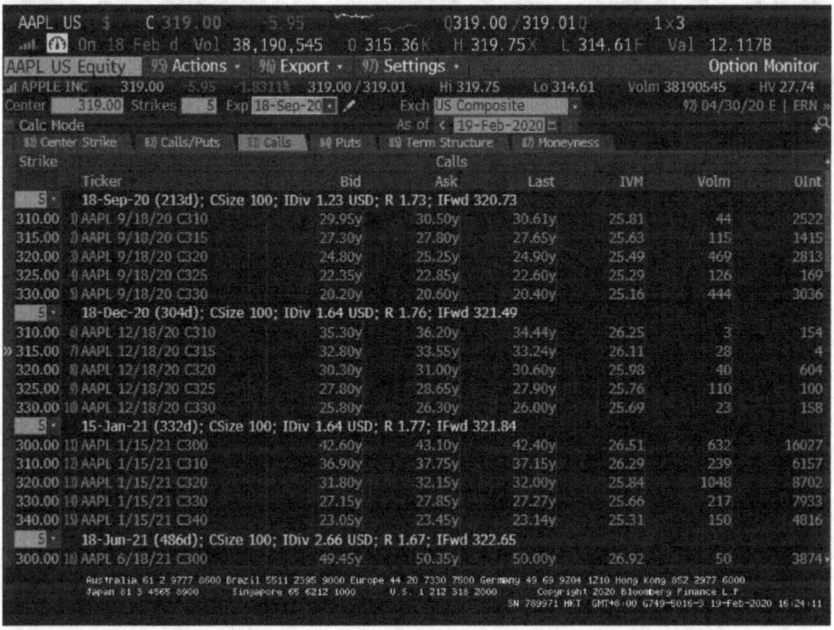
AAPL US $ C 319.00 -5.95 Q319.00 / 319.01Q 1x3
On 18 Feb d Vol 38,190,545 O 315.36K H 319.75X L 314.61F Val 12.117B
AAPL US Equity 95) Actions 96) Export 97) Settings Option Monitor
APPLE INC 319.00 -5.95 -1.8311% 319.00 / 319.01 Hi 319.75 Lo 314.61 Volm 38190545 HV 27.74
Center 319.00 Strikes 5 Exp 18-Sep-20 Exch US Composite 97) 04/30/20 E | ERN
Calc Mode As of 19-Feb-2020
81) Center Strike 82) Calls/Puts 83) Calls 84) Puts 85) Term Structure 87) Moneyness

Strike	Ticker	Bid	Ask	Last	IVM	Volm	OInt
5	18-Sep-20 (213d); CSize 100; IDiv 1.23 USD; R 1.73; IFwd 320.73						
310.00	1) AAPL 9/18/20 C310	29.95y	30.50y	30.61y	25.81	44	2522
315.00	2) AAPL 9/18/20 C315	27.30y	27.80y	27.65y	25.63	115	1415
320.00	3) AAPL 9/18/20 C320	24.80y	25.25y	24.90y	25.49	469	2813
325.00	4) AAPL 9/18/20 C325	22.35y	22.85y	22.60y	25.29	126	169
330.00	5) AAPL 9/18/20 C330	20.20y	20.60y	20.40y	25.16	444	3036
5	18-Dec-20 (304d); CSize 100; IDiv 1.64 USD; R 1.76; IFwd 321.49						
310.00	6) AAPL 12/18/20 C310	35.30y	36.20y	34.44y	26.25	3	154
» 315.00	7) AAPL 12/18/20 C315	32.80y	33.55y	33.24y	26.11	28	4
320.00	8) AAPL 12/18/20 C320	30.30y	31.00y	30.60y	25.98	40	604
325.00	9) AAPL 12/18/20 C325	27.80y	28.65y	27.90y	25.76	110	100
330.00	10) AAPL 12/18/20 C330	25.80y	26.30y	26.00y	25.69	23	158
5	15-Jan-21 (332d); CSize 100; IDiv 1.64 USD; R 1.77; IFwd 321.84						
300.00	11) AAPL 1/15/21 C300	42.60y	43.10y	42.40y	26.51	632	16027
310.00	12) AAPL 1/15/21 C310	36.90y	37.75y	37.15y	26.29	239	6157
320.00	13) AAPL 1/15/21 C320	31.80y	32.15y	32.00y	25.84	1048	8702
330.00	14) AAPL 1/15/21 C330	27.15y	27.85y	27.27y	25.66	217	7933
340.00	15) AAPL 1/15/21 C340	23.05y	23.45y	23.14y	25.31	150	4816
5	18-Jun-21 (486d); CSize 100; IDiv 2.66 USD; R 1.67; IFwd 322.65						
300.00	16) AAPL 6/18/21 C300	49.45y	50.35y	50.00y	26.92	50	3874

Australia 61 2 9777 8600 Brazil 5511 2395 9000 Europe 44 20 7330 7500 Germany 49 69 9204 1210 Hong Kong 852 2977 6000
Japan 81 3 4565 8900 Singapore 65 6212 1000 U.S. 1 212 318 2000 Copyright 2020 Bloomberg Finance L.P.
SN 789971 HKT GMT+8:00 G749-5016-3 19-Feb-2020 16:24:11

Figure 2.5: Call Option Prices of Apple Shares as on February 2, 2020

This is the page from Bloomberg for Call Options on Apple as on February 2, 2020. The shares were trading at USD 319 and different maturities are displayed separately. Besides other columns, there are columns showing Volume and Open Interest. Volume refers to number of contracts traded on that particular day and Open Interest refers to all outstanding trades. These are useful as they give an indication as to how liquid that particular contract is. For any one underlying, for different maturities and different strikes, there are several contracts possible. So each contract per se is less liquid than the underlyings.

The corresponding page for Put Options on Apple shares looks as below.

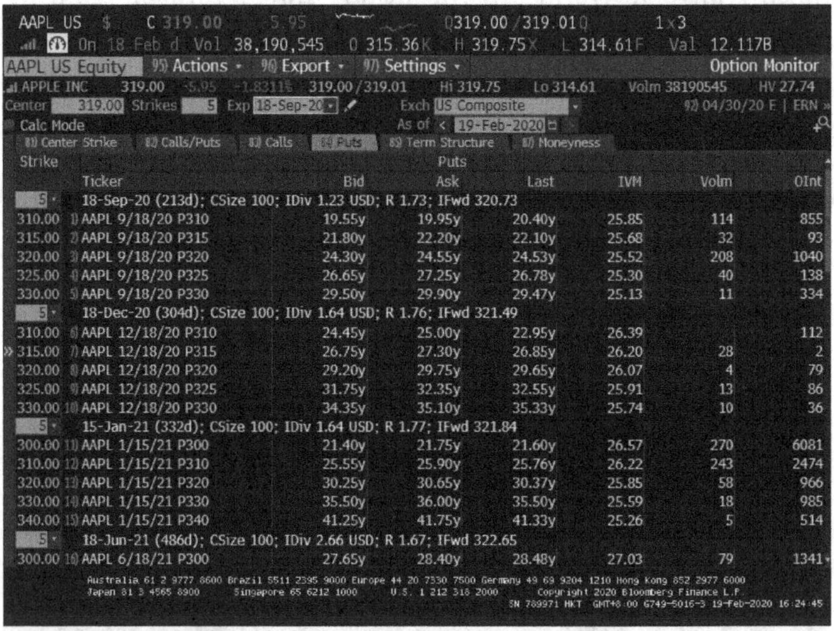
AAPL US $ C 319.00 5.95 Q319.00 /319.01Q 1x3
On 18 Feb d Vol 38,190,545 O 315.36K H 319.75X L 314.61F Val 12.117B
AAPL US Equity 95) Actions 96) Export 97) Settings Option Monitor
APPLE INC 319.00 -5.95 -1.8311% 319.00/319.01 Hi 319.75 Lo 314.61 Volm 38190545 HV 27.74
Center 319.00 Strikes 5 Exp 18-Sep-20 Exch US Composite 92) 04/30/20 E | ERN
Calc Mode As of 19-Feb-2020
81) Center Strike 82) Calls/Puts 83) Calls 84) Puts 85) Term Structure 87) Moneyness

Strike	Ticker	Bid	Ask	Last	IVM	Volm	OInt
5	18-Sep-20 (213d); CSize 100; IDiv 1.23 USD; R 1.73; IFwd 320.73						
310.00	1) AAPL 9/18/20 P310	19.55y	19.95y	20.40y	25.85	114	855
315.00	2) AAPL 9/18/20 P315	21.80y	22.20y	22.10y	25.68	32	93
320.00	3) AAPL 9/18/20 P320	24.30y	24.55y	24.53y	25.52	208	1040
325.00	4) AAPL 9/18/20 P325	26.65y	27.25y	26.78y	25.30	40	138
330.00	5) AAPL 9/18/20 P330	29.50y	29.90y	29.47y	25.13	11	334
5	18-Dec-20 (304d); CSize 100; IDiv 1.64 USD; R 1.76; IFwd 321.49						
310.00	6) AAPL 12/18/20 P310	24.45y	25.00y	22.95y	26.39		112
» 315.00	7) AAPL 12/18/20 P315	26.75y	27.30y	26.85y	26.20	28	2
320.00	8) AAPL 12/18/20 P320	29.20y	29.75y	29.65y	26.07	4	79
325.00	9) AAPL 12/18/20 P325	31.75y	32.35y	32.55y	25.91	13	86
330.00	10) AAPL 12/18/20 P330	34.35y	35.10y	35.33y	25.74	10	36
5	15-Jan-21 (332d); CSize 100; IDiv 1.64 USD; R 1.77; IFwd 321.84						
300.00	11) AAPL 1/15/21 P300	21.40y	21.75y	21.60y	26.57	270	6081
310.00	12) AAPL 1/15/21 P310	25.55y	25.90y	25.76y	26.22	243	2474
320.00	13) AAPL 1/15/21 P320	30.25y	30.65y	30.37y	25.85	58	966
330.00	14) AAPL 1/15/21 P330	35.50y	36.00y	35.50y	25.59	18	985
340.00	15) AAPL 1/15/21 P340	41.25y	41.75y	41.33y	25.26	5	514
5	18-Jun-21 (486d); CSize 100; IDiv 2.66 USD; R 1.67; IFwd 322.65						
300.00	16) AAPL 6/18/21 P300	27.65y	28.40y	28.48y	27.03	79	1341

Australia 61 2 9777 8600 Brazil 5511 2395 9000 Europe 44 20 7330 7500 Germany 49 69 9204 1210 Hong Kong 852 2977 6000
Japan 81 3 4565 8900 Singapore 65 6212 1000 U.S. 1 212 318 2000 Copyright 2020 Bloomberg Finance L.P.
SN 789971 HKT GMT+8:00 G749-5016-3 19-Feb-2020 16:24:45

Figure 2.6: Put Option Prices of Apple Shares as on February 2, 2020

When an Option is traded on an Exchange, the Buyer and Seller do not face each other. Rather, both of them face the

Exchange. In technical parlance, both have the Exchange as their counterparty. This has implications as to who fulfills the commitment under the trade. For Exchange-traded options, the responsibility is multilateral.

The second platform for trading Options is between Financial Institutions. In case the trade is done between two Institutions outside the framework of an Exchange, such trades are called Over the Counter or OTC trades. There are standardized Agreements already in place between Institutions to ensure minimized disputes relating to trades. There is an International Body called ISDA (International Swaps and Derivatives Association), which has devised these Agreements. For OTC trades, there is no need for pre-defined contracts relating to specifics of the particular trade and virtually anything can be traded. Responsibility to fulfill the commitment on OTC trades is of two institutions or is Bilateral. Since there is no one else to back up the trade, selection of counterparty for OTC trade is very important.

CASH FLOW FOR AN OPTION TRADER

Having understood the payoffs from the Options trades, we need to familiarize ourselves with an aspect of Cash Flows. A Buyer of an Option (whether Call or Put) pays the Premium Upfront and he has no more liability. His downside is limited to the amount of Premium paid. In case he has bought a Call Option, he will be receiving the cashflows in case the underlying closes above the Strike Price. In case he has bought a Put Option, he will be receiving a cashflow when the underlying closes below the Strike Price.

The situation is a bit more complex in the case of a Seller of an Option. A Seller receives the Premium upfront. However, his liability starts from the moment he enters into the trade. On top of that, his liability is unlimited. A Seller of a Call Option is exposed to the stock price of the underlying going above Strike. Similarly, a Seller of a Put Option is exposed to the downside. A natural question is how we ensure that the Seller of an Option does not renege on his commitment. This is done by charging an initial margin. In case the trade is done on an Exchange, then the Exchange is liable to the Buyer of Option for ensuring that the Seller of an Option honors his liability. Exchanges have formulas based on past transactions and the current economic environment, which arrive at initial margin. Let us say the underlying is trading at USD 100 and the contract size is 100 shares, so the nominal value of the trade will be USD 10,000. The Exchange may specify that the Seller of an option needs to deposit 15% of the notional amount or USD 1,500 as the initial margin. As the days pass, the price of Option will move up or down. In case the Price of Option has moved up, the Seller of an Option will be required to place additional margin. This is called Mark-to-Market and could happen on a daily basis. Thus, the Seller of an Option may have to deposit a Margin several times till the Maturity date.

OPTIONS BASICS AND FCNs

In explaining the basics of Options in this Chapter, I have taken you through perspectives of both the Buyer and Seller of Call and Put Options. The reason is that once the basic concept is understood, it is easy to see the logic behind investing in FCNs. An investment in FCN is akin to selling a Put Option. The Premium received from selling a Put Option is structured by Investment Banks as Coupon of the FCN. More specifically, the Investor in an FCN is selling an 'Out-of-the-Money' Put Option. His thought process is something like this; I like Apple but at $320 a share, I think the shares are overpriced. I do not mind buying them if these were trading at $288. Rather than waiting for the price to correct to $288, which may or may not happen, let me earn a coupon. In case the shares fall below $288, I will be obliged to buy at a price of $288. But in any case, I wanted to buy these at $288.

Besides the Premium received from selling the Put Option, there is one more factor which is included in the coupon of the FCN. When we sell an Option, while we receive the Premium upfront, we are not required to pay anything to the Buyer of the Option. An Investor in FCN pays the Principal amount upfront and needs to be rewarded for that. So in addition to the option Premium, the Investor in FCN also gets interest on the Principal amount invested. In other words, the Coupon of an FCN comprises of two components: Premium from the sale of the Put Option and Interest received on the Principal amount invested.

BACK TO OPTIONS BASICS

Intuitively we can see that the option to sell Apple shares at a price of $320 should be more valuable than the option to sell them at a price of $288. So the Premium to be paid for the $320 Put Option will be higher than the Premium for the $288 Put Option. Besides the Strike Price, there are many factors which influence the Premium. However, the Strike Price remains one of the most important factors in deciding the Premium.

Let us look at the other factors which may influence the Premium. I find it easier to understand these factors from the perspective of a buyer of a Call Option. If you are interested in securing a right over Apple shares over a relatively shorter period, you will be required to pay lower Premium as compared to the situation when you wish to secure this right over a longer period. The longer the duration of an Option, the higher the Premium to be paid.

Now let us compare the situation where you buy Apple shares today vis-a-vis the situation where you buy them in six months' time. In the former, you will have to shell out the full $320 per share upfront, whereas in the latter you can earn interest on your $320 for the next six months. Naturally as a buyer of a Call Option you need to compensate the seller for this interest earned by you. On the other hand, if you had purchased Apple shares on day one, you would have received Dividends over the next six months. So the Seller of the Option needs to compensate you for the loss of your ability to earn these Dividends.

Normally, the effect of interest rates and Dividend is captured in the Futures Price of the asset. The price of any liquid asset in Futures market is quite straightforward and can be depicted as below.

Forward Price = Spot Price + InterestDividend– Borrowing Cost

While calculating the Premium for a Call, rather than considering two factors (Interest and Dividend), it is easier to use Futures Price of the underlying asset.

The factors discussed above which affect the Premium can be summarized as below.

1. Strike Price versus Initial Price
2. Duration
3. Interest Rate
4. Dividend

VOLATILITY

This brings us to the final factor influencing the Premium: volatility of the stock. As explained above in Figure 2.1, as a Buyer of a Call Option we want the prevailing price of Apple Shares to be above our Strike Price. For the sake of simplicity, let us assume that we have bought a Call Option with a strike of $200 and maturity of six months. Let us look at the following two situations.

Table 2.1: Prices of Apple Shares under Two Scenarios

	Scenario 1	Scenario 2
Month 1	295	290
Month 2	298	293
Month 3	311	315
Month 4	305	312
Month 5	307	295
Month 6	309	318

In case the price of Apple shares fluctuates as shown in Scenario 1, the chances of them crossing the Strike Price are lower than the chances if Apple shares were to fluctuate as per Scenario 2. The price of Apple shares has crossed $310 only once in Scenario 1 whereas it has crossed $310 three times in Scenario 2. So price is more volatile in Scenario 2 as compared to Scenario 1. Higher volatility increases the chances of our Call Option being 'in money'. Naturally we need to pay a higher Premium for this privilege. The higher the volatility of the stock, the higher the Premium to be paid.

If we plot a graph with Prices of the stock on x-axis and the number of times that price occurred during a given time period, the graph looks like a bell-shaped distribution curve. Please note the shape of the two graphs in Figure 2.7 and 2.8.

In the Figure 2.7, we see less extreme prices and also fewer instances of extreme prices. The curve is narrower. As against this, the graph Figure 2.8 has more extreme readings and the number of such readings is higher. Naturally, the prices in the second scenario are more volatile. If we juxtapose the instances of low, medium, and high volatility in one single graph, it will look like Figure 2.9.

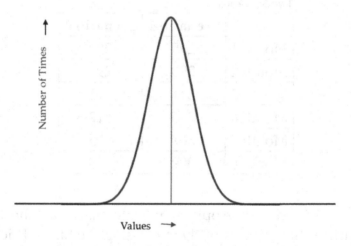

Figure 2.7:   Distribution of Prices in Scenario 1

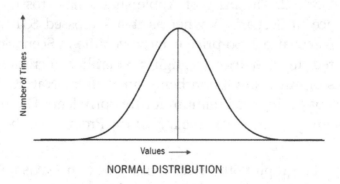

Figure 2.8:   Distribution of Prices in Scenario 2

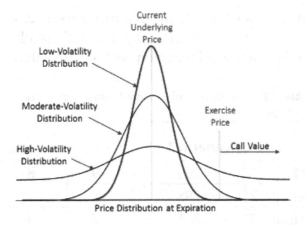

Figure 2.9: Distribution of Prices Under Different Volatility Scenarios

The highest point of these curves is the Mean, which also represents the current price (Forward Price to be more precise). All three scenarios in Figure 2.9 represent a normal distribution and there is an equal likelihood of the share price of Apple being 10% higher or 10% lower from the current price. Since we have bought a Call Option on Apple at a Strike Price of $300 when the prevailing price was $280, the number of observations above $300 are highest in the graph with highest volatility. So the chances of Apple shares being above $300 are highest in the graph with higher volatility.

Like the share prices, the volatility of the share prices also change on an ongoing basis. The mathematical basis of calculation of volatility is Standard Deviation. The formula for the calculation of Standard Deviation is as below:

$$SD = \sqrt{\frac{\sum \left(p_i - p_{avg} \right)^2}{(n-1)}}$$

The share prices of Apple in Scenario 1 were 295, 298, 311, 305, 307, and 309. The average or mean of these observations is 304. So the Standard Deviation will be calculated as below:

Table 2.2: Calculation of Standard Deviation of Prices of Apple Shares

	Scenario 1 (p_i)	$P_i - P_{avg}$	$(P_i - P_{avg})^2$
Month 1	295	−9	81
Month 2	298	−6	36
Month 3	311	+7	49
Month 4	305	+1	1
Month 5	307	+3	9
Month 6	308	+4	16
		Total	192

Standard Deviation = $\sqrt{192/(6-1)}$ = 6.196

The Standard Deviation calculated above is the Monthly one. Similarly, we could calculate the Standard Deviation by using daily prices. However, Volatility is defined in terms of annual variation. Since there are 260 working days in a year, it is customary to multiply the daily Standard Deviation by the square root of 260 to arrive at the figure of annual Volatility. This standardization helps in comparing Volatility across different time periods. For example, we may be calculating Volatility using the prices over one month or six months, so the process of annualizing makes the comparison easy. We can say that the Volatility of this stock over the past three months is 20, or we can say that its Volatility over the past six months is 25, and everyone will understand that we are talking about annualized Volatility.

HISTORICAL VOLATILITY VERSUS IMPLIED VOLATILITY

We calculated the Volatility of Apple above using the prevailing prices in the month of June 2019. More precisely, we calculated the volatility of daily returns of share price of Apple. Since we used historical data as the base, we have calculated the Historical Volatility of Apple. However, what we are interested in is the future value of the option and not in the past value. For this we need to estimate the future expected volatility. There can be several considerations in this calculation. Many market participants are using different parameters to arrive at their estimate of future volatility. These participants then use these estimates to trade-in options. Many of the options are traded on Stock Exchanges. So we know the Market view for the value of any given option. Since most of the determinants of price of an option (except future expected volatility) are relatively easy to decide, and since there is more or less a consensus on these, we can do a back calculation to arrive at a figure which represents the market view of future volatility. This figure is called Implied Volatility, or simply what the volatility we can imply from the market prices of traded options. In Figures 2.5 and 2.6 above, the column with heading IVM gives this figure for Options on Apple stock.

We will see later as to how we can benefit from this market estimate of future volatility.

EUROPEAN OPTION VERSUS AMERICAN OPTION

Having covered the factors influencing the Premium, we need to understand the kind of right we are buying. If our Call Option is giving us the right to buy Apple shares at a price of $310 only at the end of six months and not at any time in between, it is known as the European Option. On the other hand, if we can exercise this right at any time during the intervening six months, it is known as the American Option.

It is possible that Apple shares are trading at $315 in three months' time. If we are holding an American Call Option, we can oblige the Seller of the Option to deliver us Apple shares at a price of $310 on that very day without waiting for another three months. In practice, since there is an unexpired period of three months, you can sell the Call Option to someone else. From the perspective of this new buyer, he is buying a Call Option to buy Apple shares in three months' time at a Strike of $310 when the prevailing price is $315. This difference between the prevailing price and Strike Price is known as the Intrinsic Value of the Option. You will not oblige the Seller of a Call Option to deliver you shares but will make more profit by selling a Call Option. Of course, there are some exceptions but we can ignore them for the time being.

When an Investor invests in an FCN, he is selling a European Put Option. He is offering to buy Apple shares at a price of $288 only at the end of six months. He is immune to the price of Apple shares during the intervening period. The only material price for him is the price on the Final Observation Day. If the price on that day is below Strike Price, the Investor gets the delivery of Apple shares. If the price of Apple shares on the Final Observation Day is above the Strike Price, the Investor gets his Principal back. Coupon is in any case paid.

Chapter 3

HOW TO CONSTRUCT A FIXED COUPON NOTE (FCN)

Usually, FCNs are created by Product teams in Wealth Management Firms. They will come up with an idea and the Relationship Managers will reach out to their clients. A typical product marketed by Wealth Managers has three underlying stocks usually from the same sector. For example, all three underlyings are either from Technology or Financials. The communication from the Relationship Manager will say something about the attractiveness of the sector and the Investor can choose to invest as much as he wishes. This is something like buying off-the-shelf products. A typical Investor tends to overlook not only the finer points like frequency of auto-callability, but even the selection of underlyings is not paid due attention. Many a time, the proposal will have two good stocks and the third stock is such that the Investor is only vaguely familiar with it. Since the Investor is carrying the risk of getting the delivery of the worst performing stock, due attention needs to be paid to the stock selection. In fact, the Investor should think that he is going to buy that very stock and proceed only if he is comfortable with the stock.

STOCK SELECTION

Many Investors start with maintaining a list of stocks which they like and work from that list to create FCNs. In case the Investor prefers a top-down approach, he would like to start with country, sector, industry, etc. and then move to identifying specific stocks. Most Wealth Managers publish their yearly, monthly, and weekly views of the economy and markets along with the sectors where they are overweight or underweight. They also publish their research on stocks which are covered by them and the ratings of each of these stocks. Some of the stocks have 'Buy' ratings, whereas other stocks have 'Hold' or 'Sell' ratings.

In the financial world, two types of research are prevalent: Sell Side or Buy Side. Sell Side research means that the primary interest of the Publisher is in selling his services. This research is done by big brokerages who are usually part of big Investment Banks. These analysts would be meeting the management, gathering information from other stakeholders like customers, suppliers, competitors etc. They will be attending conference calls with the management and ask them the right questions. They will analyze the Business Models and competitive landscape, and will project future revenues, costs, and profits. Then they will build mathematical models like Discounted Cash Flow (DCF) and will come up with a Fair Value. Fair Value when compared with the current market price will result in specific rating like 'Buy' or 'Sell'. They will also publish their target price.

In the old days, the brokerages used to earn revenues when their clients used to act on their information and place orders. However, with the unbundling of services following new

MIFID (Markets in Financial Investments Directive) Rules, brokers have to charge for their research separately. The most important clients of these brokerages are Institutional Investors like Asset Managers, Insurance companies, or Sovereign funds. Besides the information provided by the brokerages, they also value the access to the Management provided by the brokerages. For example, a Fund Manager would like to meet the Management before deciding to take a position in that particular stock. Due to the importance of information, analysis, and the access to the Management, brokerages are valued highly by their clients. Sell Side analysts have their remuneration linked to the revenue generated on their recommendation. For example, some recommendations may make a client trade more. These analysts will be rewarded whether the recommended stock performed as he predicted or not. The ratings given by Sell Side analysts are all collated on Bloomberg Analyst Recommendation or ANR Page.

As against Sell Side analysts described above, Buy Side analysts generally do not make their research available to third parties. Typically, they would be working for an asset management firm or an Insurance Company. They usually depend on the research of Sell Side analysts and build their own models. Their job includes identifying the best Sell Side analysts for a sector or a company. They will be building on the work already done by the Sell Side analysts. Most of the Wealth Mangers will be having their own Buy Side analysts who would be publishing their research for the benefit of their clients. The Buy Side analysts will usually be rewarded based on the performance of the stock recommended by them. Unlike the Sell Side analyst, their remuneration does not depend on the turnover generated by their employer. In fact, in some of the Wealth Management organizations, almost

60% of the remuneration of a Buy Side analyst is variable and is dependent on the performance of the stock recommended by him. Such an analyst wants his recommended stock to perform and hence his interest is much more aligned with that of the Investor.

For an Investor who is starting to invest in FCNs for the first time, this research is a good starting point. Such an Investor would be well advised to obtain Buy lists from his Wealth Manager. It would be better still if the Investor can access recommendations made by more than one Wealth Manager. Just to clarify, these are the stocks which are recommended by the Wealth Managers for buying at today's prices. Considering the fact that the Buy Side analysts working for Wealth Manager have already built upon the research provided by the Sell Side Analysts, there is some merit in their recommendations.

ACCEPTABLE PRICE

The Investor may identify the stocks which appear in the Buy lists of more than one Wealth Manager. A stock which appears on the Buy list of more than Wealth Manager will generally be a good stock to have. The next step can be a Fundamental Analysis of these stocks. While factors like Revenue growth, Return on Equity, etc. are important, particular attention needs to be paid to factors like Price to Earnings ratio or Price-to-Book ratio. The reason is that though the identified company is very good in terms of quality, we do not wish to be exposed to an overvalued company. The aim should be to identify good companies which are available at a decent price. We also need to consider the Target Price given by Wealth Managers. Let us say that Apple is trading at $320 and the Target Price is $352. So the analyst is predicting a 10% upside to the stock. Since we are identifying the stock for the purposes of FCN, which will have a Strike of around 80%, there will be a safety buffer of 20% from the current price. This will mean that in the worst-case scenario, the Investor may have to buy Apple shares at a price which will be 30% below the Target Price.

Figure 3.1 is the ANR Page from Bloomberg of Apple. From the top left panel, we can see that the consensus rating of Apple on that day was 4.04. These ratings are derived from the ratings given by Analysts who have updated it in the past 12 months. Buy is assigned a rating of 5 and Sell is assigned a rating of 1. The closer the rating is to 5, the stronger is the conviction of Analysts to buy that stock. In this case, 59.6% of Analysts have a Buy and 31.9% have a Hold rating. Below

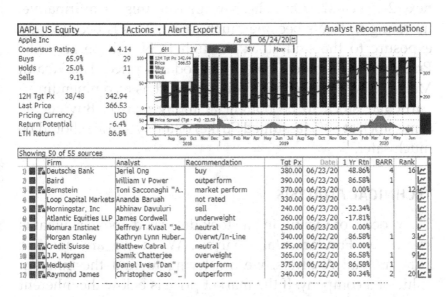

Figure 3.1:   Analyst Recommendation Page on Apple as on February 19, 2020

Source: Bloomberg

this is the 12-month Price Target of $336. This is the average Price Target given by Analysts in the past three months. The top right panel shows how the recommendations have evolved over the past two years. This gives the percentage of analysts giving a Buy rating, consensus target price, and also the prevailing prices at those points in time. It is interesting to note that as the share price of Apple was going up in the second half of 2019, the percentage of Analysts giving a Buy rating was also going up. The bottom Panel gives the details of individual Analysts covering the stock, their respective target prices, their performance in the past, and their ranking.

Having gone through this analysis, the Investor will be ready with the stocks which he does not mind being exposed to. The Investor may think, "Do I mind holding this stock for the next 2–3 years?" Once he can answer this in affirmative, investing in FCNs become much easier. This is because any exposure to the said stock through FCN will be at Strike Price, which is much lower than today's price. The Wealth Manager, who has a reputation to protect, is recommending a particular stock to be bought at today's price. Buying the same stock at 80% (assumed Strike) of today's price should be much safer.

TECHNICAL ANALYSIS

The process of identifying a stock described above is what is known as Fundamental Analysis. When we are doing a Fundamental Analysis, we are trying to find the inherent value of a company. If the market price is below the inherent value, the stock can be bought and vice versa. Technical Analysis also tries to find the undervalued companies, but the approach is through the study of Charts. It may not be a bad idea to apply the tools of Technical Analysis to the stocks identified through Fundamental Analysis.

Generally there is a belief that Technical Analysis is useful only for short-term market timing, and when we invest in FCNs, we would generally be investing for six months or longer. However, Technical Analysis can be employed for identifying long-term trends as well. When we are using Technical Analysis to identify market entry or exit points, we tend to look at daily price charts. When we are trying to identify long-term trends, it is better to use weekly or monthly charts.

There are some patterns on long-term charts which can help in identifying the trends. More particularly, we need to look for trends which help in identifying the stocks which have a bearish pattern. Since an Investor in FCN does not stand to share the upside, he needs to avoid the downside as much as possible.

A Head and Shoulder pattern appearing on a long-term chart means that the stock is likely to go down. Even if a stock looks attractive on a Fundamental basis, the current price being close to the Neck Line should make an Investor think about the appropriate entry point. It may be a better idea to wait till the stock corrects and bounces from support level before the same is considered for FCN.

By the same logic, a reverse Head and Shoulder pattern should give comfort regarding the current price being a good entry point.

Like the Head and Shoulder pattern, Double or Triple Top should make an investor cautious about the entry point. Double Top looks a bit like the Head and Shoulder pattern with the difference that there are only two peaks. A break of the trough line means that the stock is due for a significant correction. Naturally this will not be the best of times for selecting the stock for an FCN.

A descending triangle pattern has progressively lower tops and flattish bottoms. A break through the bottom line generally means that stock will go down.

Other patterns which indicate a bearish signal include a bearish wedge and bearish rectangle.

DIVIDEND

Dividends are paid out of cash available to the company. Typically, a company which has a high Dividend pay-out will have a dip in share price on ex-Dividend date (the first day of trading after dividend has been paid out). Another way to look at the situation is that the share price of such a company is unlikely to go up that much. Since FCNs are a play only on the share price, when we have an underlying with a high Dividend pay-out ratio we should go in for a lower strike.

SHARE BUYBACK

When we have a choice of doing FCN on two underling companies which are identical, save for the expected share buyback announced by one of them, we would naturally prefer a company which has an ongoing share buyback program. This is because the share buybacks are expected to increase the share price and FCNs are a play on share price alone without any regards for any other feature like Dividends.

IMPLIED VOLATILITY

Once the Investor has made up his mind regarding the stocks he does not mind being exposed to, the next step is to wait for the right volatility. We have covered this concept in the previous Chapter. An Investor in FCN is selling a Put Option on the underlying stocks. One of the important determinants of Premium to be received on the sale of an Option is the Volatility. More specifically, it is the Implied Volatility rather than the Historic Volatility. Implied Volatility is the figure which market participants are using to calculate the Premium on an Option. In other words, Implied Volatility is the price the Buyers of the options are willing to pay. Buyers of the Put Options pay the Premium mainly because they wish to protect against losses due to fall in prices of their holdings. In other words, they are insuring their positions against a fall in value beyond certain level.

If we think outside of the stock world, when do people buy Insurance? Insurance is most appealing just after any catastrophe. It is a basic tenet of human nature that we are driven by Greed and Fear. When the Fear is high, let us say after a natural disaster, there are more people willing to insure themselves. These are the times when Insurance companies not only get more inquiries and sell more policies, they also typically increase their Premia. Since most people understand that an Insurance Company has had to pay a higher amount for the previous disaster, they also understand that the Insurance Company has to jack up the premia for the coming year. Imagine a time when no natural disaster has happened for past several years, there will not be many people interested in buying the Insurance. Moreover, the Insurance Companies will not even think of raising the premia for the coming period. Similarly, you would generally think of increasing the Medical coverage when someone in your circle has recently faced some serious illness.

The position of a Seller of a Put Option is akin to an Insurance Company. As an Investor, you may think, "All my life I have been buying Insurance, how can I sell Insurance. I do not wish to be exposed to losses if any untoward thing happens." If such thoughts come to your mind, you should think whether Insurance Companies are profitable. In reality, Insurance is one of the most profitable sectors of the economy. Of course, if Insurance policies are sold without a careful analysis of the Risk, any Insurance Company will go bankrupt. Similarly, if you sell Insurance for inadequate Premium, you may not be profitable enough. So the key thing in selling Insurance is to understand the Risk and take only that much Risk that you can live with.

As a Seller of a Put Option or as an Investor in FCN, we need to ensure that the Risk is what we are comfortable with and we are getting rewarded for that Risk. Unlike an Insurance Company, which has fixed overheads and hence is obliged to always provide a quote for Insurance, an Investor in FCN has the flexibility to be in the business only during the times of his choosing. The Investor would have already identified the Risk he is willing to take. The identified stocks are nothing but the sector in which an Insurance Company is engaged. For example, a particular Insurance Company may be insuring medical expenses, another may be insuring life, third one may be insuring property and so on. The Investor would have already decided that he wishes to consider particular sector like

Financials or stock like Bank of America. As an Insurance Company decides that it will not sell Medical Insurance to persons over 70 years of age, the Investor has decided that he does not mind buying Bank of America at 75% of today's price. The next most important consideration is what reward he is getting. Just as the Buyers of catastrophe Insurance are willing to pay more after a natural disaster, the Buyers of a Put Option on Bank of America are also willing to pay more after a recent fall in its share price. As explained in the previous chapter, Volatility goes up when there is a sudden, large movement in the share price. It does not matter whether the price has gone up or down. For example, see the chart below of Volatility of Facebook share price during January–February 2019.

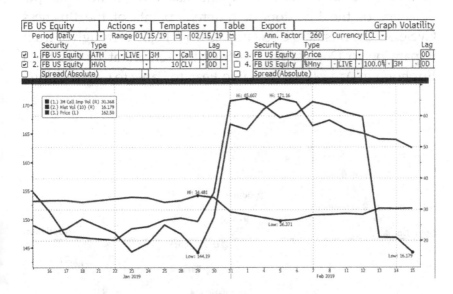

Figure 3.2: Volatility of Facebook Stock

The share price went up from a low of USD 144.19 on January 29 to a high of USD 171.16 on February 5. This resulted in a spike in Historical Volatility but Implied Volatility came down sharply. This means that the holders of this stock were not willing to pay higher premia for insuring against the fall in the price of Facebook shares.

Volatility as defined in statistical formula goes up in both the cases, whether the share price goes up or down. If we input the value of Historical Volatility in Black-Scholes formula, the result will be higher Premium even in the cases when the share price has gone up recently. However, these are not the times when the buyers of Put Options will be willing to pay for the Insurance. They will be willing only when there is fear in their mind.

Behavioral Finance as a discipline has thrown light on the behavior of the Investors at different points of the Business Cycle. As the Business Cycle moves from Peak to Trough or from Expansion to Depression, the Investor sentiment moves from Euphoria to Anxiety, to Denial to Fear, to Panic to Capitulation.

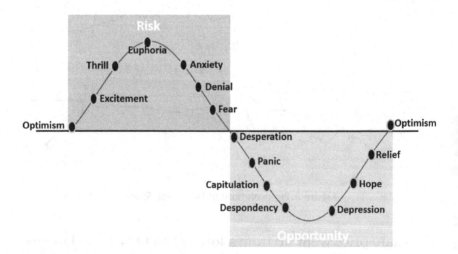

Figure 3.3:   Movement of Investor Sentiment with Business Cycle

Figure 3.4: Movement of Consumer Confidence with S&P 500

The Chicago Conference Board has been tracking consumer sentiment for the past several decades. If we see the chart of this Conference Board Index with the S&P 500 index, we can see that Consumer Confidence clearly follows the level of the S&P 500. When the level of S&P 500 goes up, Consumer Confidence also goes up. Similarly when the level of S&P 500 goes down, Consumer Confidence also goes down. The Chart above shows the movement of two indices during the period 1996 to 2008 and the Chart below shows the same movement from 2008 to 2019.

Now Consumer Sentiment is one thing and willingness to pay for the Insurance against the fall in prices of Equities may be another thing. Volatility Index, popularly known as VIX, is an index which tracks the Implied Volatility for the near-month options on S&P 500. Here the correlation is even

Figure 3.5:   Movement of Consumer Confidence with S&P 500

Figure 3.6:   Movement of VIX (Inverted Scale) with S&P 500

clearer. As the level of S&P 500 goes down, the amount the Investors are ready to pay for Insurance goes up.

Some Investors follow the steps whereby they first identify the stocks they do not mind being exposed to and ascertain the Implied Volatility of these stocks. This is especially easy for the stocks which have listed options. Generally, an Implied Volatility above 20 means that the returns from FCNs will be meaningful.

These are the times when the Investor in FCNs or the Seller of a Put Option starts exploring the opportunities. In such times, he benefits not only from the willingness of the market to pay more but also from the fact that due to the fall in price of stock, the Strike is even lower. Let us say that we started looking at Bank of America when the share price was $30. Due to panic in the market, the price has corrected to $25. Assuming that the Investor was comfortable with 75% strike, due to a fall in share price, his actual Strike Price will now be $20 instead of original strike of $24. So he is has a lower Risk and is getting a higher reward.

A NOTE ON VIX

For an Investor in FCNs, VIX plays an important role by signifying the Implied Volatility at the level of S&P 500 index. The level of VIX is frequently reported in Financial Press. When there is a market turmoil, VIX shoots up and Investors get to read about this in the Press. VIX is the short form for Volatility Index. This index was started by the Chicago Board Options Exchange (CBOE) in 1993. As the name suggests, this Exchange is the primary venue for trading Options. While the NYSE (New York Stock Exchange) and the NASDAQ

(National Association of Securities Dealers Automated Quotations) are the primary Exchanges for trading Equities in the USA, CBOE is the primary Exchange for trading Options. In fact, among all countries, USA is the one with the most liquid Option market. Broadly, three types of Options are trades on CBOE: Indices, Individual Stocks, and Interest Rates. This trading of Call and Put Options in S&P 500 index forms the basis of calculating VIX.

Initially, VIX was calculated on the basis of prices at which 'at the money' Call and Put Options were trading. The duration of these Options was one month. This meant that VIX did not represent the Implied Volatility for 'out of the money' Options. Generally, an Institutional Fund Manager is able to tolerate some degree of fall in the value of his portfolio. He may be willing to buy protection if the value falls below 90%. For such a Buyer, the relevant level is not 'at the money'. He is interested in buying Put Options which are 'out of money' by 10%. Similarly, an Investor who is holding an Equity portfolio may be willing to give away upside beyond 110% of the value. For him the relevant level of Implied Volatility is the one which represents Call Options which are 'out of money' by 10%. In order to take care of the interest of such parties, who actually outnumber those who wish to trade 'at the money' Options, the calculation of VIX was modified to include 'out of the money' Options.

The way it is done is that the traded mid-prices of all the Options for different Strikes are taken into account. Let us say that S&P 500 index is trading at 2800 level, the prices of all options with Strikes of 2800, 2795, 2790, ... onwards and 2805, 2810, 2815 onwards will be taken into account. In case there are no prices for two consecutive Strike Prices, no further Strike Price is taken into account. Let us say that Option prices are available for 1600, 1595 strikes and are not available for 1590 and 1585 strikes. This will mean that prices for strikes 1580, 1575 onwards will not be taken into account. Since VIX is calculated daily, it is possible that these prices may become available tomorrow. When the prices for 1590 and 1585 become available, the series beyond that will also be taken into account. As the market volatility increases, the breadth of Strike Prices of traded Options also increases. For example, let us say that before March 2020, the lowest Strike traded Put Option on S&P 500 was 1200, it is possible that strike of 1000 starts trading in April 2020. This can affect the calculation of VIX.

We should also be mindful of one more characteristic of VIX. When an Investor invests in FCN, typically he will invest for six months or one year. So he is selling a Put Option of six month or one year duration. So the relevant level of Implied Volatility for him is for six months or one year. As against this, VIX denotes the Implied Volatility for one month (actually maximum 37 days). Due to the effect of Volatility Term Structure, which will be discussed in Chapter 5, Implied Volatility of longer duration should usually be higher.

CHARACTERISTICS OF VOLATILITY

Volatility is usually mean reverting, which means that after a period when it is elevated above the normal levels, it comes back to normal levels. This is very different from prices of stock. A particular stock or a particular index can continue to rise and may not come back to the previous level. For example, from the time when S&P 500 touched 600 in March 2009,

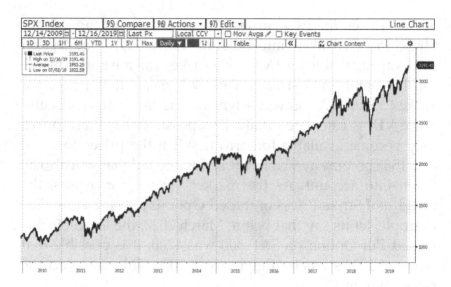

Figure 3.7: Movement of S&P 500 from 2009 to 2019

it has risen to 3370 in February 2020. It has not gone back to the 600s since then. If we look at the ten-year chart, the lowest level was 1022 on July 2, 2010 and it has risen to 3370 on February 18, 2020.

As against this, as we can see from Figure 3.8, volatility of S&P 500 has been ranging between 10 and 20 for most of this period. Periods of low volatility are followed by periods of high volatility. Similarly, periods of high volatility are invariably followed by periods of low volatility. This Figure depicts the volatility based on prices over past 100 days. We can see from the top right box that annualized factor of 260 has been used to calculate annual volatility.

The Volatility Index of the Chicago Board of Options Exchange, more popularly known as VIX, is the index

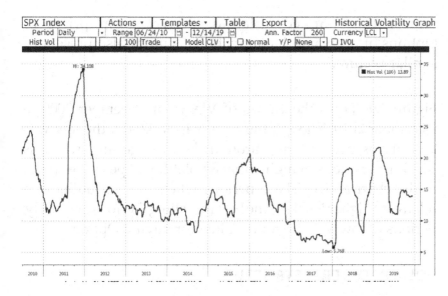

Figure 3.8: Volatility of S&P 500 from 2009 to 2019

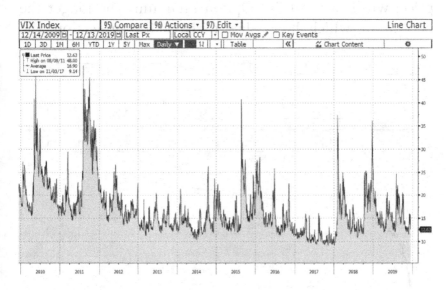

Figure 3.9: Movement of VIX from December 2009 to December 2019

representing Implied Volatility derived from prices of Options of near-month contracts. This index also presents a similar picture.

Figure 3.9 shows the values of VIX from December 2009 to December 2019. Though the high was 37.32 and the low was 9.14, it has been moving around the average line, which is 14.50. The periods of high implied volatility appear like spikes in the chart above. These periods when VIX is trading at a relatively higher level are the best for selling Options. Similarly, periods of low VIX are more suited for buying Options.

VOLATILITY TERM STRUCTURE

A Portfolio Manager who wishes to protect his portfolio against a fall in the value of portfolio is willing to pay a price, which we call Put Option Premium. The longer the period for which he wishes to have the protection, the

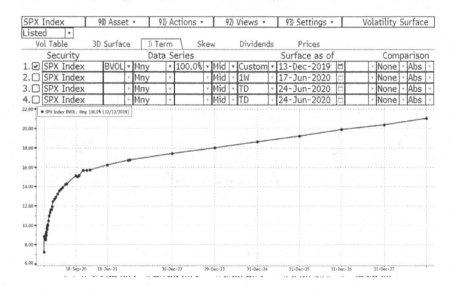

Figure 3.10:   Volatility Term Structure

higher the price he has to pay. We have already noticed that 'time' is one of the determinants of the price of Option Premium. But is the Premium actually proportional to the time? In real life, the Premium is higher for longer duration options. This is captured in the values of Implied Volatilities for different durations. As the time period increases, Implied Volatility increases up to a certain point and then flattens gradually. Implied Volatility of S&P 500 for different periods is depicted below.

VOLATILITY SKEW

Now let us say the portfolio manager has decided that he wishes to buy the protection for one year. He is also required to decide the level below which he needs the protection. There may be a portfolio manager, who is risk averse and does not wish to take a loss of more than 5%. Or there may be a portfolio manager who does not want to pay too much for the protection

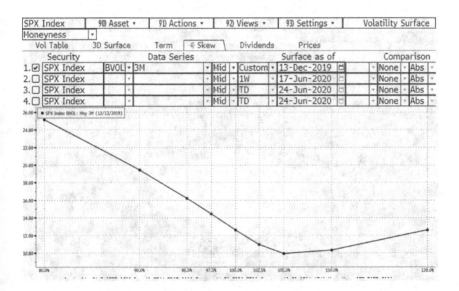

Figure 3.11: Volatility Skew

and thinks that his clients will forgive him for a fall in the value of up to 20%. Any loss more than 20%, and his clients will take their money away from him. When we consider on a proportionate basis, the second portfolio manager will be required to pay more as the Options for Strikes of 80% are more expensive as compared to Options for Strikes of 95%. This feature of Implied Volatility is depicted on a graph as below.

While the Implied Volatility for a strike of 100% is 12.65, it increases to 26 for Strike of 80%. Naturally, the Option to protect the portfolio from a downfall of 20% will be more expensive on a proportionate basis.

VOLATILITY SURFACE

For Option traders it is easier to visualize the Term Structure and Skew of Volatility in one single graph. This graph is known as Volatility Surface.

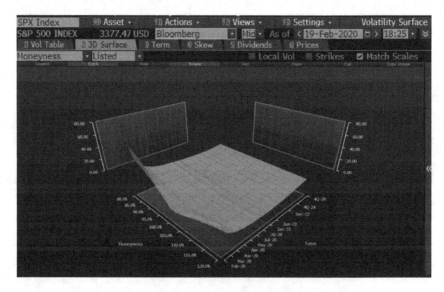

Figure 3.12: Volatility Surface

An Investor in FCN is interested in maximizing the Premium to be received from the sale of a Put Option. As the Implied Volatility is higher for Strikes around 80% and for durations which are slightly longer, he would try to go in for these levels.

CORRELATION

Having discussed the concepts of stock selection and timing of trade, let us consider a typical FCN marketed by Wealth Managers. It is very common to have all the underlyings from a single sector. Sectors could be banking, pharmaceutical, energy, utilities, etc. For example, one FCN may have Bank of America, Citigroup, and J. P. Morgan (all being US Banks) as underlyings. Another one could have Facebook, Alphabet, and Microsoft (all being US Technology Stocks) as underlyings. Such FCNs make it easy for the Relationship Managers at the Wealth Management Firm to market it. The pitch will be something along the lines of, "interest rates are going up in the USA and this will increase the Net Interest Margin for the Banks. So the share prices of Banks are likely to go up". An Investor needs to be aware of two aspects of this practice. One, this approach leads to the underlyings which have been proposed by the Wealth Manager, rather than underlyings which are the first choice of the Investor. Second, this approach leads to underlyings with high correlation. Investing based on current themes has the advantage of simplicity but takes away the advantage that comes with low correlations amongst the underlyings.

The reason why Wealth Managers do this is that it makes it possible for them to create one single Pitch Book, which is easy to market. If the underlyings were from different sectors, multiple reasons will be required to justify the Product. Simple reasoning means less work for the Wealth Manager.

Correlation is a statistical concept which shows the prices of two or more stocks in relation to each other. Let us say that on average, the stock price of Stock A moves up by 1%, how much does the price of Stock B move? Let us look at the following Chart which shows the correlation of Citigroup and Bank of America for the period August 2018 to July 2019. As we can see from the top panel, the correlation has moved between 0.80 to 0.87. It is visually easier to see from the bottom panel that the two stock prices move in tandem.

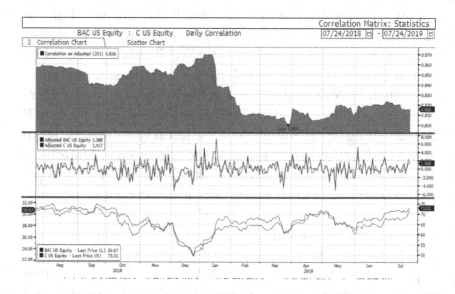

Figure 3.13:   Correlation of Stocks of Bank of America and Citigroup

Against the correlation between Bank of America and Citigroup, let us look at the correlation between Johnson & Johnson and Facebook. The correlation has moved between 0.09 to 0.20. The bottom panel also shows that the two stocks move on their own.

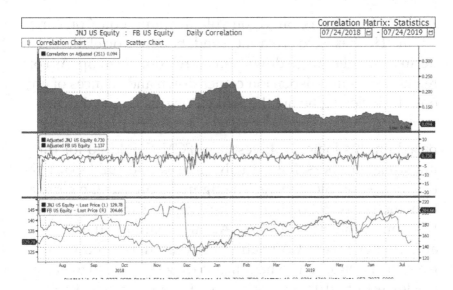

Figure 3.14: Correlation of Stocks of Johnson & Johnson and Facebook

Can the two assets have a perfectly negative correlation of 1? That would mean that when asset A goes up by 1%, asset B goes down by 1%. Though it seems unlikely, there is one area where such perfect negative correlation exists. An example will be S&P 500 ETF (exchange-traded fund) and Short S&P 500 ETF.

When the underlyings have high correlations, the Investor does not get the benefit in the form of lower Strike or higher Coupon. So while the risk carried is of three stocks, the reward is equivalent to doing an FCN with one underlying. One possible line of thought for the Investor is to think, "I am comfortable with all three underlyings and ultimately I can be delivered only one underlying, so I may as well invest in an FCN with three underlyings. This way I get rewarded for the risk of three while actually I am ultimately exposed to the risk of one underlying".

An FCN Investor is 'Short' on volatility and 'Long' on correlation. He has sold volatility and bought correlation. He desires volatility to go down and correlation to go up. As correlation goes up, dispersion comes down and chances of any one stock closing below the Strike Price also come down.

Based on this logic, an Investor in FCN should go for three uncorrelated stocks. It is actually quite easy to build a correlation matrix on Bloomberg. The figure below has the correlation matrix of following stocks: Apple, Bank of America, Johnson & Johnson, Danone, Airbus, Tencent, HDFC Bank, and Toyota Motor. Correlation between these stocks varies from the highest of 1 (when the two stocks move together) to the lowest of –0.02. Let us say we have identified Apple as one of the underlyings and wish to ascertain two other stocks for FCN. We can see that Danone and Toyota have the lowest correlation with Apple. So we are likely to get better pricing if we do an FCN on Apple, Danone, and Toyota.

1) Edit	2) Actions ▾	3) Add Matrix Shortcut	4) Settings				My Correlation Matrices: Matrix		
07/24/2018 ▦ - 07/24/2019 ▦			Daily		▾	Calculation	Correlation ▾	Local CCY ▾	
<Filter>				Correlation Matrix (10 Rows x 10 Columns)					
Security	AAPL	BAC	JNJ	BN	AIR	700	HDB	7203	C	FB
11) AAPL	1.000	0.457	0.294	0.090	0.395	0.207	0.231	0.139	0.521	0.446
12) BAC	0.457	1.000	0.194	0.061	0.327	0.187	0.220	0.183	0.816	0.265
13) JNJ	0.294	0.194	1.000	0.159	0.213	0.099	0.148	0.065	0.257	0.094
14) BN	0.090	0.061	0.159	1.000	0.378	0.140	0.225	-0.025	0.133	0.035
15) AIR	0.395	0.327	0.213	0.378	1.000	0.247	0.219	0.128	0.415	0.179
16) 700	0.207	0.187	0.099	0.140	0.247	1.000	0.257	0.219	0.213	0.084
17) HDB	0.231	0.220	0.148	0.225	0.219	0.257	1.000	0.072	0.269	0.181
18) 7203	0.139	0.183	0.065	-0.025	0.128	0.219	0.072	1.000	0.168	0.056
19) C	0.521	0.816	0.257	0.133	0.415	0.213	0.269	0.168	1.000	0.331
20) FB	0.446	0.265	0.094	0.035	0.179	0.084	0.181	0.056	0.331	1.000

Figure 3.15: Correlation Matrix

High correlation between a bunch of stocks means that their performance will have lower dispersion, and vice versa. While constructing FCNs, we are looking for stocks which have low correlation and hence high dispersion. Let us consider two baskets of stocks: one with low dispersion and one with high dispersion. Let us assume that the mean returns of both the baskets are the same. Graphically, these baskets are depicted in Figure 3.16.

In the case of Basket A, the chances of any stock closing below 90% of the initial level are lower. So a Buyer of a Put Option on the 'worst of' this basket will not be willing to pay much to insure against losses below 90%. As against this, in the case of Basket B, the worst performer is expected to close below 90% of the initial level. Hence a buyer of a Put Option on the 'worst of' this basket will be ready to pay more. Since an Investor in an FCN is a Seller of a Put Option on 'worst of' a basket of stocks, he stands to earn a higher Premium in case of Basket B. By adopting this strategy, the Investor is 'long' correlation versus the Buyer of the Option, who is 'short' correction. Since higher volatility of individual stocks also leads

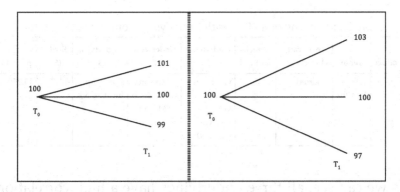

Figure 3.16: High Correlation/Low Dispersion versus Low Correlation/High Dispersion

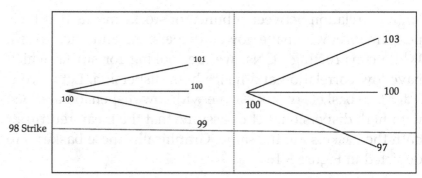

How Low Correlation among Underlyings increases the probability of at least one underlying closing below the Strike

Figure 3.17:   High Dispersion Increases the Probability of Underlyings Breaching the Strike

to higher dispersion, both the parameters (higher volatility and lower correlation) are complementary to each other.

A NOTE OF CAUTION

Please see the pricing of a one year, quarterly autocallable FCN on three of the largest US Banks. This pricing was valid on May 5, 2020.

Table 3.1:   Pricing of an FCN with Underlyings from the Same Sector

Product	Tenor	Autocall Observation	Knock-Out (%)	Underlying 1	Underlying 2	Underlying 3	Strike (%)	Coupon p.a. (%)
FCN	12 Months	Quarterly	100%	Goldman Sachs Group Inc/The (GS UN)	JPMorgan Chase & Co (JPM UN)	Citigroup Inc (C UN)	60.00%	13.25%

As we can see, all three underlyings have a high correlation and the Product should benefit when a non-correlated or less

Table 3.2: Pricing of an FCN with Underlyings from Different Sectors

Product	Tenor	Autocall Observation	Knock-Out (%)	Underlying 1	Underlying 2	Underlying 3	Strike (%)	Coupon p.a. (%)
FCN	12 Months	Quarterly	100%	Goldman Sachs Group Inc/The (GS UN)	JPMorgan Chase & Co (JPM UN)	QUALCOMM Inc (QCOM UQ)	60.00%	12.57%

correlated stock is added to underlyings. So Citigroup was replaced with Qualcomm.

However, the new combination resulted in a lower Coupon. The reason is that Citigroup had a much higher Implied Volatility as compared to Qualcomm. So the effect of higher Implied Volatility was stronger than the effect of low correlation. This means that we should not go in for uncorrelated stocks straightaway, but see whether the effect of Implied Volatility is higher than the effect of correlation.

AUTOCALL FEATURE

Besides selecting stocks with higher Implied Volatility and lower correlation, having an Autocall feature is another way to enhance yield on an FCN. This feature means that on each Observation Date, if the underlying stock closes above certain level, the trade expires, and the Investor receives his Principal back along with the Coupon. Let us take the case of a one-year FCN with quarterly Observation Dates and which is autocallable if all the underlyings close above the initial level. In the event all the underlyings close above the initial level at the end of Quarter 1, the Product will have life of only one quarter.

One may think that instead of the risk of the Investor continuing for 12 months, it is coming to end in three months, so the reward should be lower. Rather than higher Coupon, autocallable feature should lead to lower Coupon. However, we must note that such a feature leads to higher Coupons only when the condition is that 'all the underlyings' should close above the initial level. The condition is not that 'any one of the underlyings' should close above the initial level. The difference is that in the case of the former, all the underlyings have gone up as compared to the initial level. So, the chances of the Product maturing with one of the underlyings below Strike level have gone down. In such a case, why should the Buyer of a Put Option pay Coupons for the remaining period of the Product? The buyer of a Put Option is happy seeing his expected liability towards Coupon payments for Quarter 2, Quarter 3, and Quarter 4 extinguish. So he rewards the seller of a Put Option by paying higher Coupon for a trade with an autocallable feature.

The seller of a Put option would have been happier to continue with receiving the Coupons in a situation where all the underlyings have gone up from the initial level. However, he traded this preference for a higher coupon for Quarter 1. He can always look for other trades when the initial Product is autocalled. However, he would be running the re-investment risk. He may not get an equally attractive FCN but that is the choice he made when he initially entered the trade. Obviously, in the case of a Product which is autocallable monthly rather than quarterly, the Investor is running the risk several times more. Naturally the reward for a monthly autocallable FCN will be more than a quarterly autocallable FCN.

Having an autocall level of 110% of initial level means fewer chances of the Product being autocalled and hence higher chances of receiving Coupons. So Issuers will usually quote higher Strikes when autocall is at 110%.

COUPON BARRIER

This feature means that coupons are payable only if all the underlyings close above a certain predefined level. This level could be same as the Strike level on maturity or it could be different. Since the Coupons become conditional on the fulfilment of a given condition, the Product can no longer be called a 'Fixed Coupon Note'. An FCN technically means that coupon is paid under all circumstances. A Note with conditional Coupon may be called a Phoenix (the reason is that as a phoenix rises from ashes, a Phoenix Note may not pay Coupon for one quarter but may pay Coupon for the next quarter). Nevertheless, since other features of an FCN remain the same it is useful to be aware of this yield enhancement possibility.

Having a barrier for the payment of the Coupon means that probability of the Coupon payment goes down. Hence the Investment Bank must compensate the Investor by paying a higher Coupon.

QUALITY OF THE ISSUER

An Investor in an FCN like any other Structured Product carries the risk of the Issuer of the Product. A lower quality Issuer may be obliged to compensate the Investor by offering a higher Coupon or lower Strike. However, in case anything going wrong with the Issuer, the Principal amount itself may be at risk. The counterparty needs to have the ability and intention to honor their obligations on the Coupon payment dates as well as on maturity. Hence it is better not to play around with this feature and it is advisable to stick to the highest quality Issuers. The Investors should also be aware of this feature when they compare the prices provided; apples need to be compared to apples and not oranges.

CURRENCY

Some aspects of choosing the denomination currency of FCNs have already been dealt with in Chapter 1. The currency in which the Investor invests in FCN should ideally be the same as underlyings. For example, if the underlyings are all USA stocks, usually the FCN will be denominated in USDs. However, there are situations where the underlyings trade in a currency different from the reference currency of the Investor. For example, let us say the Investor's reference currency is USDs and he likes European underlyings like BNP Paribas, BMW, and Inditex. Or there could be a situation in which the Investor likes underlyings which trade in different currencies like Euro, JPY, and HKD. Such structures are called Quanto, which is a short name for 'Quantity Adjusting Option'. While investing in a Quanto structure, the Investor is exposed to both the variation in stock price of the underlying as well as variation in currency.

In the case of a USD denominated FCN on European stocks, this is how the payoff will work on maturity. In case the underlyings close above Strike, the Investor gets back his Principal and Coupons. In case any one of the underlyings close below Strike, the Strike Price in Euros will first be converted into USDs. Let us take the following example.

Trade Date: September 26, 2018
Initial Euro/USD: 1.17
Underlyings:

Name	Initial Spot	Autocall Level	Strike Price
ABI	76.94	76.94	63.0831
BMW	77.76	77.76	63.7554

Let us say that on maturity, BMW closes at Euro 58.70 and the final Euro/USD rate is 1.10. As a first step, the Strike will be converted into USDs: Euro 63.7554*1.10 = USD 70.13. Let us say the Investor had invested USD 250,000 in FCN. He will get 250,000/70.13 = 3564 shares of BMW plus USD 57 cash. Since the initial USDs invested are now worth more in Euros, the Investor has benefitted from the depreciation of Euro but has been at a disadvantage due to the fall in the price of Euros. He would have been worse off if the Euro had appreciated against USD and BMW had fallen in price.

If the same Investor had converted his USDs into Euros on day one, he would have gotten Euro 213,675. On Maturity, he would have got 213,675/63.7554 = 3351 Shares. By investing in USDs, he would have benefitted from the depreciation of Euros and gotten a higher number of shares.

In a nutshell, the Investor needs to be aware of the currency risk he is carrying and be ready to take appropriate steps should the trade start going against him.

QUARTERLY RESULTS

The Investor should also be aware that volatility of stock prices is usually higher around the dates of quarterly results.

It is not a bad idea to avoid having the maturity date close to the date of quarterly results.

FCN VERSUS LISTED PUT OPTION

Very often, Investors wonder if it is better to go in for selling a Put Option which is listed or whether FCNs offer better a Risk Reward. In order to answer this question, we need to be aware of the following:

• Not all stocks have listed options which are traded. Generally, US stocks have listed Options while European and Japanese stocks either do not have listed Options or the liquidity in these is very poor. However, Wealth Managers can obtain quotations on most of the stocks in the OTC (Over the counter) market.

• When we sell a Put Option, we get the Premium upfront. As against this, Coupons in FCNs are paid at the end of the month or quarter.

• An FCN Investor is required to part with the amount invested upfront. The sale of a Put Option entails blocking a margin. This margin could be the lending value of a Fixed Income Portfolio. In case the client is not utilizing this lending value, there is practically no investment upfront. However, while calculating returns, the Investor needs to be mindful of the Risk. The returns should be calculated in terms of Risk and not in terms of Amount Invested.

• In FCNs it is possible to do 'worst of' structures, which enhance yield. Such possibilities do not exist for listed Options. As explained above, there are other possibilities like Autocall feature or conditional Coupon feature to enhance yield in the case of FCNs.

• In the case of an FCN, the Investor is bearing the counterparty risk. In the case of listed Options, the risk is of the

Exchange. Naturally the risk of Exchange is lower than the exposure to a single counterparty.

- In the case of listed Options, Implied Volatility is the chief driver of returns. In the case of FCNs, besides volatility, correlation/dispersion of the underlyings contributes significantly towards returns. In addition, interest on amount invested also plays a role.
- When an Investor sells a Listed Put Option, he has a part of the assets in his account blocked as margin. Usually the margin has two components: initial margin and Mark-to-Market margin. Initial Margin is calculated by Exchanges and usually Wealth Manager may add some additional requirements. Let us say we are doing the following trade:

Sell Put Option
Underlying: Apple Shares
Initial Price: USD 320
Strike Price: USD 280
Premium Received: USD 10

The Exchange may require that 10% of this amount, or USD 28, must be kept by the Broker with the Exchange as initial margin. As the price of the underlying goes down, the price of the Put Option will change. Let us say that Apple goes down to USD 270. The Put Option may now be worth USD 20. The difference of USD 20 and USD 10 must also be kept with the Exchange. So when we sell Listed Options, we need to be prepared to post additional margin requirements. The inability to meet this requirement can result in the position being squared up by the Broker.

So in the case of a sale of a Put Option, the downside of the Option Seller is unlimited. Let us say when we sell a Put Option on Apple of Strike 280, the downside can be all the way to zero. Such an eventuality, though unlikely, is not impossible. Peabody Energy used to be the biggest coal company in the world till 2016. The company went into Chapter 11 bankruptcy and emerged with the equity value of existing shareholders totally wiped out. Someone who had sold a Put Option on 100,000 shares with a Strike of 15 had to incur a loss equal to the notional value of trade. He may have placed an initial margin of USD 225,000 only for the trade. As against this, an Investor in FCN can incur a maximum loss equal to the amount invested initially. No further amount can be called from him.

So, in the case of an FCN, the Investor need not worry about the margin to be posted. He can never lose more than the amount he invested initially.

HOW TO IMPROVE THE STRIKE FOR AN FCN

Sometimes the Investor is faced with a situation where he wishes to invest in an FCN, has identified the underlyings, but he does not find the pricing attractive. What I mean by pricing is that either the Strike is not good, or the Coupon is not attractive enough. In simple words, there is not enough reward for the risk being taken. Most of the time it happens when Implied Volatility is not high enough. These are the times when there is complacency and counterparties do not feel the need to hedge their positions to the downside. However, these are the times when a typical Fixed Income Investor is gathering the courage to move towards Equities. Like other walks of life, there are no free lunches in the field of investments. If an Investor wants a higher Coupon, he has to be prepared to give up something else.

There are some possibilities for an Investor who wishes to improve the Coupon of an FCN.

1. **Extend the Tenure**: Instead of a typical tenure of six months or one year, the investor can think of extending the tenure to two or three years. As this will mean that the Investor is exposed to the Risk for a longer period of time, there are ways to mitigate the Risk. One can bring in the Autocall feature. This will increase the chances that the Product will not last the full three years. It is also possible to have quarterly autocall levels at progressively lower levels. For example, a three-year product could have auto-call at the end of the first, second, and third quarters at 100%, 97.5%, or 95%.

2. **Go in for Uncorrelated Stocks**: Let us say that an Investor is comfortable with 10 different stocks from 5 sectors and 3 different regions. Instead of clubbing stocks from the same region or sector, trying a combination from different regions and sectors will usually result in a better Coupon.

3. **Increase the number of Underlyings**: Instead of the usual three underlyings, one can think of five or six underlyings. There is no limit on the number of underlyings. However, the additional underlyings need to be uncorrelated or less correlated. Having more underlyings which have high correlations will not improve the Coupon.

4. **Increase the Frequency of Autocall**: As we increase the frequency of autocall, let us say monthly autocall instead of quarterly autocall, the Issuer's Risk is reduced. This happens because should the underlyings have all gone up, the Issuer has less need to hedge his position to the downside.

5. **Knock-In**: It may be possible for an Investor to accept a higher Strike, provided the chances of reaching that particular Strike are reduced. This can be achieved by having a Knock-In feature. This feature means that until and

unless one of the underlyings trades below Knock-In level, the Strike is not relevant. However, in case the Knock-In level is breached, then the Investor will be delivered the stock at Strike Price. Knock-In can be European, which means that it will be observed only on maturity. Let us say that we have a Strike of 90% with a Knock-In of 65. In the event on the Final Observation Day, one of the underlyings closes at 60, the Investor will have to buy the stock at 90. This will mean a loss of 30 when compared to the prevailing price. Since the probability of stock trading below 65 is lower than its probability of trading below 90, the Investor has traded the lower probability for higher potential loss.

An even more aggressive strategy will be to go in for American Knock-In. This means that none of the daily close should be below 65. As the chances of an underlying closing below 65 on a daily basis are much higher, the Issuer has to reward the Investor suitably.

6. **Make the Coupon Conditional**: As the Product is called 'Fixed Coupon Note', the Coupon is usually fixed or guaranteed. This guaranteed feature means that the Issuer has to honor the payment of the Coupon under all circumstances. Naturally, the Issuer needs to be rewarded for undertaking this commitment. And the reward is usually higher Strike. If we make the coupon conditional on certain events happening, the FCN can be structured with a lower Coupon. The conditional event could be that all underlyings could close above certain level. For example, a Product having a Strike of 80% could have a 'Coupon Strike' of 70%, which means that Coupons will be paid only if all underlyings close above 70%.

Chapter 4

PERFORMANCE EVALUATION AND REMEDIES

Having invested in a Fixed Coupon Note (FCN), continuous monitoring of the position is as important as monitoring an Equity position. Typically, an Investor would be checking the prices of his Equity holdings either several times a day or at least once a day. A similar level of alertness is required regarding FCN positions. An Investor should not treat this position like a Fixed Income position where the movement on a day to day basis is not very significant. This is so both from the Risk Management perspective and also from the performance evaluation perspective. The first way to keep track is to simply watch the Bank statement provided by the Private Bank or Wealth Manager. These statements are available online and can be viewed anytime as per the convenience of the Investor. However, the Investor must be aware that the prices of various securities are not real time but are updated once a day.

The feed for these prices is provided by the Issuing Institution to the Wealth Manager, who in turn applies the updated prices to the portfolio of the Investor. We need to be aware of the factors affecting the prices on a daily basis:

1. **Coupon Accrual Date**: Let us say that we have invested in a one-year FCN with a Coupon of 8% p.a. and the frequency of Coupon payment is quarterly. As the quarter progresses, assuming other factors remain the same, the price of the FCN increases by the amount of Coupon accrued. On the day before the Coupon accrual day, the price of the FCN can be 102%. Usually an FCN, especially the one with autocallable feature, will not have a price higher than this.

2. **Underlying Prices**: This is the most important factor in determining the price of the FCN. In case one or more of the underlyings start going down in price, it will start reflecting in the price of the FCN almost immediately. However, the relationship is generally non-linear. This is so because there are other factors affecting the price of the FCN. Nevertheless, any deterioration in the price of the FCN should make us aware of the Risk. We need to start preparing for any remedial action required.

3. **Volatility of Underlyings**: As we discussed in Chapter 2 on Options basics, Implied Volatility of the underlying is the most important factor affecting the price of an Option. Generally, any dip in the price of the underlying will make market participants be agreeable to pay more for the protection and hence increase the Implied volatility. So in a way, this factor is linked to the price of underlyings.

4. **Dividend**: In case an increase in Dividends leads to a drop in ex-dividend price, it can again have an adverse impact on the price of the FCN.

5. **Interest**: An FCN is basically a Note, which is akin to a Bond. Any increase in interest rates depresses the Bond prices and vice versa. Similarly, a reduction in interest rates can have a positive effect on the price of the FCN. Fixed Income Investors are aware of the concept of 'Duration', which is the weighted average of future returns. The longer the Duration of a Bond, the larger is the effect of a given change in interest rates on the price of a Bond, As a rule of thumb, a 1% increase in the interest rates will have the effect of reducing the price of a Bond with a Duration of one year by 1%. Usually FCNs have a tenure of less than two years and given the low duration, movements in interest rates usually do not have significant impact on the prices of FCN.

6. **Credit Quality of the Issuer**: As the price of a Bond will go down with deterioration in the credit quality or rating of the Issuer, the price of an FCN can go down should the credit quality of Issuer go down. An FCN issued by Lehman Brothers would have gone down in value significantly in September 2008.

USEFULNESS OF PRICING

The price of an FCN as reflected in the Bank Statement of an Investor, while not being exact, serves several useful purposes:

A. It is a fairly good indicator of the price at which it can be wound down. Let us say that having invested in the FCN, the Investor either gets uncomfortable with the Risk or needs liquidity. As such, the price of the FCN gives an indication of the price at which it will likely be wound down.

B. This price is what is taken into account by the Wealth Manager to calculate the lending value of the portfolio. Let us say that the lending value of an FCN is 60%. It means that the lending value is 60% of the price being reflected in the Bank Statement. As this value goes down, there may be shortfall in the lending value and there may be a situation of Margin Call. When we were comparing FCNs to selling Put Option, we noticed that the sale of Put Option will be subject to a daily Mark-to-Market (MTM). As against this, an Investor in FCN does not have to worry about daily MTM. This is true if the Investor invests in FCN without taking leverage. If he uses his own money to invest in an FCN yielding 8% and underlyings go down below Strike, there will still be no Mark-to-Market and there cannot be a Margin Call. However, the situation will be different if the Investor has borrowed from the Bank to invest in an FCN which is going down in value.

C.   This price is an important Risk Management tool. As soon as the prices of underlyings start going south, the price of the FCN will start reflecting this. So any fall in the price of the FCN must awaken the Investor about the possible risk in future. However, this should be taken as the initial warning signal and we must have better risk monitoring tools to do a proper Risk monitoring.

RISK MANAGEMENT

This is the most important part of the Investment process. Whether the Investor invested in an FCN, as it was marketed by his Wealth Manager, or based on his own preferences, Risk Management is required in both situations. The most practical way is to watch the performance of the share prices of underlyings. This movement can affect the prices of FCNs directly and also as a consequence of increase in Implied Volatility. A simple Excel file with the following columns can help in this monitoring, as seen below.

Once investment has been made in an FCN, the details can be added in a new row. Only the values in the last two columns

Table 4.1: A Sample Table for Tracking an FCN Portfolio

Description	Underlying	Bloomberg Ticker	Initial Spot	Strike Price	Last Price	" Last Pr/Strike
8% 6 Months FCN Strike 82.22%	Airbus Group NV	AIR FP Equity	118.8	97.6774	117.70	20%
	BNP Paribas	BNP FP Equity	44.54	36.6208	42.33	16%
8% 6 Months FCN Strike 81.55%	AstraZeneca PLC	AZN LN Equity	61.83	50.4224	70.09	39%
	LLOYDS BANKING GROUP PLC	LLOY LN Equity	0.6302	0.5139	0.51	-1%
	Reckitt Benckiser Group PLC	RB/ LN Equity	62.95	51.3357	61.99	21%
8% 6 Months FCN Strike 80.5%	BP PLC	BP/ LN Equity	5.784	4.6561	5.02	8%
	British American Tobacco	BATS LN Equity	31.09	25.0275	28.07	12%
	Diageo plc	DGE LN Equity	31.34	25.2287	33.20	32%
8% 1 Year FCN Strike 70.57%	Amazon.com Inc	AMZN UQ Equity	1852.4	1307.2387	1,705.51	30%
	Citigroup	C UN Equity	67.58	47.6912	66.40	39%
	Comcast Corp	CMCSA UQ Equity	41.29	29.1384	44.11	51%
8% 1 Year FCN Strike 52.92%	Align Technology Inc	ALGN UQ Equity	309.3	163.6816	184.30	13%
	Alphabet Inc-CL A	GOOGL UQ Equity	1079.95	571.5095	1,190.13	108%
	Micron Technology Inc	MU UQ Equity	34.01	17.9981	42.64	137%
8% 1 Year FCN Strike 64.03%	Alexion Pharmaceuticals Inc	ALXN UQ Equity	117.11	74.9855	95.80	28%
	Bank of America Corp	BAC UN Equity	28.17	18.0373	27.63	53%
	Facebook Inc	FB UQ Equity	178.65	114.3896	177.75	55%
8% 1 Year FCN Strike 72.65%	Goldman Sachs Group INC	GS UN Equity	194.79	141.5149	197.37	39%
	Intuitive Surgical Inc	ISRG UQ Equity	530.11	385.1249	509.00	32%
	Microsoft Corp	MSFT UQ Equity	136.77	99.3634	135.67	37%
8% 1 Year FCN Strike 77.70%	Reliance Industries Ltd	RIGD LI Equity	36.15	28.0886	36.50	30%
	ICICI Bank Ltd	IBN UN Equity	11.53	8.9588	11.67	30%
	Infosys Ltd	INFY UN Equity	10.96	8.5159	11.12	31%

change on a day to day basis. The values in all other columns remain static during the life of an FCN. As the prices of the underlyings get updated on a day to day basis, we need to monitor the distance between the prevailing price and the Strike Price. As the prevailing price starts to come closer to the Strike Price, we need to get alert regarding the possibility that this FCN may result in the delivery of the underlying.

Since an Investor in an FCN has written a Put on the worst of three underlyings (usually), he needs to focus on the worst performing stock. While there can never be a full certainty as to which of the three stocks will be delivered to the Investor, we need to keep the following factors in mind.

In times of a drastic correction in the market, the correlation amongst the stocks goes up and all the stocks tend to move together. Imagine a situation like September 2008, since all the stocks were going downhill at a rapid pace, identifying which stock will be the worst performing at the time of maturity will be difficult.

Let us take the example of the second FCN in Table 4.1. The details of this FCN are as below.

Trade Date: April 9, 2019
Final Valuation Date: October 25, 2019

Table 4.2: Details of an FCN for Tracking Purposes

Name	Initial Spot	Strike Price
AstraZeneca PLC	61.83	50.4224
Lloyds Banking Group	0.6302	0.5139
Reckitt Benckiser	62.95	51.337

As time progressed, while the share prices of AstraZeneca and Reckitt Benckiser went up, the share price of Lloyds Banking Group started going down. So much so that it was around 0.49 as on August 14, 2019. This drop meant that the FCN was likely to result in the delivery of shares of Lloyds Banking Group. So some remedial action was required.

As a first step, the Issuer was approached for squaring up the position. However, the Issuer quoted a price of 92.80, which meant the loss of Principal of USD 7.20 and also accrued interest of USD 0.60 or a total loss of USD 7.80. Another possibility was buying a Put Option on Lloyds Banking Group. This Option was being quoted as below:

Strike: 0.50
Maturity: October 25, 2019 (Final Observation Date of FCN)
Premium: 0.029 (Or 5.80%)

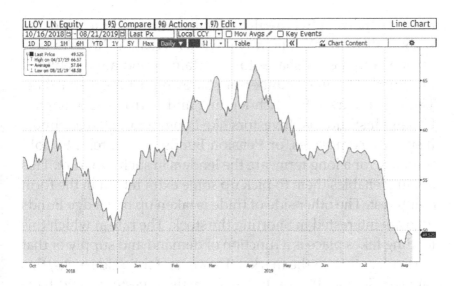

Figure 4.1: Price Chart of Lloyds Banking Group

This possibility meant that the Coupon for the remaining period of USD 1.42 would also be received.

As compared to unwinding cost of USD 7.80, buying a Put Option meant a cost of USD 4.38, so this Put Option was purchased. Since the Coupon of USD 2 for the first quarter had already been received, the net loss on trade worked out to USD 2.38. This loss was preferred over the possibility of the share price of Lloyds Banking Group going down further.

The other possible remedial action could be to Short the stock. The logic is that this particular FCN is likely to result in the delivery of the stock and the Investor would be owning the stock on the maturity date. There is a likelihood that the price of that particular stock may go down in the intervening period. So you may as well sell the stock before you get the delivery. The position can be squared up when the Investor gets the delivery.

Most of the reputed Wealth Managers are able to lend the stock to their clients. The way it works is that the Investor borrows 'x' number of shares for a certain period and is obliged to return the same number of shares on a pre-agreed date. There is a market for such lending and borrowing of shares. Usually Institutional Investors like Long/Short Hedge Funds, Insurance companies, or Pension Funds, who intend to hold the stock for a long term, are the lenders in such a market. This lending enables them to pick up some extra return in the form of interest. The other side of trade is taken up by Hedge Funds who are interested in Shorting the stock. The rate at which this lending takes place is a function of demand and supply of that particular stock in the market. However, for liquid stocks, this rate is as low as 1% p.a. In any case, the Investor would have chosen such a stock as underlying for his FCN for which there is sufficient daily turnover on the Exchange.

The Wealth Manager, having lent the stock, would require the Investor to place a Margin which can be used in case the stock price starts going up. The initial margin is usually 105% of the value of stock. This margin can be in cash or in the form of US Treasury. As the Investor would be borrowing the stock with the purpose of selling, 100 out of total requirement of 105 will be financed out of that. The balance has to be funded by the Investor. This balance can be in the form of loanable value of other securities in the portfolio. Hence the total cost of borrowing is usually limited to just 1% p.a. As the Investor would be borrowing the stock only when some time has lapsed in the life of the FCN and probably 2–3 months are left the actual nominal cost of borrowing is less than 1%.

The advantage of this Risk Management Strategy over Squaring Up the FCN or buying a Put Option is that it entails lower costs. Once the Investor has borrowed and sold the stock, he is hedged against any further fall in the price of the underlying. However, he is exposed to any increase in the price of the underlying over the Strike Price. In such a case, he will not get the delivery of the stock, and he will have to cover his Short position. Nevertheless, the fact that the FCN trade has been done for a Coupon of 8% means that the Investor has some room to play around. One possibility is to Short the stock when it goes below 2% from Strike and buy back the stock when it goes 2% above Strike. However, frequent buying and selling of the stock will entail transaction costs. So there cannot be a fixed solution for such a situation. Depending on the view on the stock at that point in time, appropriate decision can be taken.

In the example above, the share price of Lloyds Banking Group went above the Strike Price and the Investor would have been required to cover his Short position.

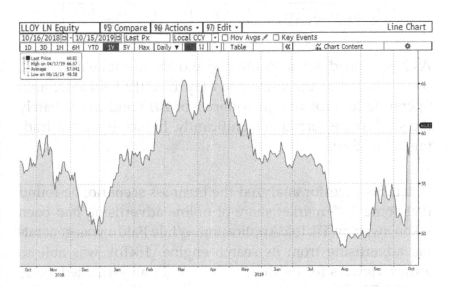

Figure 4.2: Price Chart of Lloyds Banking Group

In situations where the share price oscillates across Strike Price several times, this solution will require trading multiple times and transaction costs will build up. We need to keep in mind that when the Investor decided to invest in a particular FCN, the underlying hypothesis was that he was prepared to hold it, provided the cost to him was below the Strike Price. Still, it is possible that the situation has changed and the Investor is no longer bullish on the prospects of the delivered underlying. In such a situation, there are some possible solutions.

Let us see one more example. The Investor invested USD 300,000 in a 9.40%, 12-month FCN on February 11, 2019 with the following underlyings.

Table 4.3:   Details of an FCN for Tracking Purposes

Reference Asset	Initial Price	Strike Price
Prudential Finance	91.59	64.1130
Baidu Inc	172.22	120.5540
Microsoft Corp	106.03	74.2210

As it happened, while Prudential and Microsoft held up well, Baidu started losing value. On May 17, 2019 Baidu declared operating loss for the first quarter of 2019 and immediately the stock price corrected significantly. In fact, it started trading below Strike.

When the Investor analyzed the business scenario, he found that some 20% market share of online advertising had been taken away by TikTok Application. While Baidu was generating advertising from its search engine, TikTok was able to attract viewers for its short videos. With an estimated value of USD 75 billion, its parent company ByteDance became the

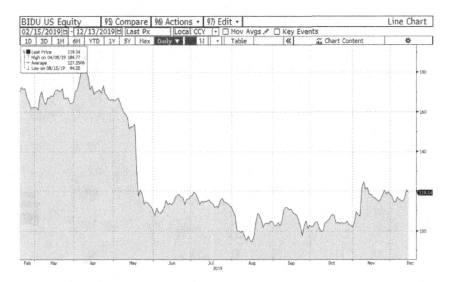

Figure 4.3: Share Price of Baidu

most valued non-listed company in the world. Most of the analysts became bearish on the stock of Baidu.

When the Investor weighed the possibility of buying the Put Option, the Premium was quite high. The Investor decided to keep a watch and continue with the position. The mental calculation was that the Investor would be receiving a Coupon of USD 28,200 and he would end up with 2,488 shares of Baidu. So his cost per share excluding the interest would be USD 109. The Investor was prepared to forego the interest earned and decided that he would Short the stock if it dropped below USD 109. He had checked that the stock was available for borrowing at a low cost of 1% p.a. As things progressed, Baidu went down to USD 94.

Baidu announced the Quarter 3 2019 results on November 7, 2019 and the stock went above 109. The Investor bought the

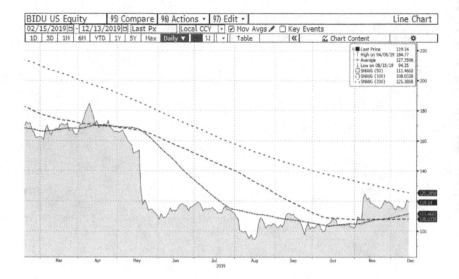

Figure 4.4:   Share Price of Baidu

shares and squared up his Short position. As things progressed, Baidu crossed the 50-day moving average on the same day and the Investor did not feel the need for taking any other remedial action.

The main point of this discussion is that in situations where we are certain that only one of the three underlying stocks is going below the Strike Price, we can hedge the position by Shorting the stock. The idea is that we can return the borrowed stock when we get the delivery on the maturity of the FCN. The risk in this strategy is that in case the stock goes above Strike, we may not get the delivery of the stock. Thus we need to monitor the stock price with carefully planned Limit order to buy back the stock.

TECHNICAL ANALYSIS

Usually Technical analysis is considered useful in market timing. There are indicators which show when an Index or a particular stock is close to breakout or is nearing its support level. When an Investor takes the initial position, he needs to be careful not to select stocks which have broken their support level. Similarly, Technical Analysis can be quite useful when the investment in an FCN has already been made and the product is showing signs of stress due to correction in the prices of one or more underlyings. Such an analysis can make the decision whether to hold on to the FCN or to go in for Shorting the stock much easier.

RECOVERY NOTES

Should an Investor land up with a stock upon maturity of an FCN, there are some Structured Products which can help in reducing the losses.

DIGITAL NOTE

By 'Digital' we mean that it is in an 'either' 'or' state like zero or one. This type of Structured Product can be done even in circumstances where there was no previous FCN. However, it is especially useful in the circumstance when an Investor has been delivered the underlying. Now the Investor wishes to recover his losses, which are already substantial. He thinks that the share price will improve, but not so much as to reach his cost price.

So the Investor sells the shares received at the prevailing price and invests the sales consideration in a new Digital Note. This is not a capital protected Note, which means that at the end of its tenure, the Investor will receive the same number of shares but these may be trading at a lower price than today.

On maturity of the Product, say at the end of six months, if the share price moves up even slightly, the Investor will

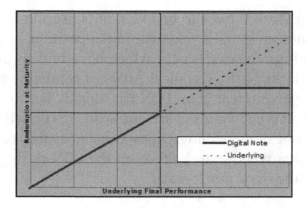

Figure 4.5: Pay-off Diagram of a Digital Note

receive a pre-decided coupon. To take a concrete example, an Investor was delivered shares of BNP Paribas on February 14, 2019. The prevailing price was Euro 40.415. A six-month Digital Note done that day gave a Coupon of 25% flat. So in case BNP closed at or above Euro 40.415 on August 28, 2019, the Investor would get a return of 25%. As it turned out, BNP closed at 40.20.

So even though BNP was trading above the level of Euro 40.20 in the intervening period, the Investor did not benefit. In fact, he lost out on Dividends of Euro 3.02 paid during this period. Simultaneously, he got the same number of shares back, which he had originally.

In the example above, the level at which the 'Zero or One' event happens is the current price of stock on the day the Digital Note is traded. However, this level, which is known as Strike Price, need not necessarily be at the current price. It is possible to have Strike Price higher or lower than the current price.

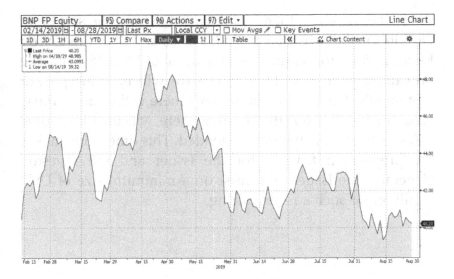

Figure 4.6: Price Chart of BNP

BONUS COUPON NOTE

A Bonus Coupon Note is similar to a Digital Note except that in the case the underlying closes above the initial price, the Investor gets to participate in the upside up to a certain point.

CANCEL AND REBOOK (RESTRUCTURE)

Another possibility is to get the Note restructured before its maturity. Let us say that there is a market event and the underlyings are trading significantly below the Strike Price. The Investor feels that it is a temporary event and the prices will recover. He can approach the Issuer to restructure the existing FCN into a new FCN. The new FCN may either extend the tenure of the Note, may change the Strike, or may change other features. Usually the Issuer will try to accommodate such requests. When we extend the tenure, and keep the Strike the same, there will be a value from the sale of an Option for the extended period. Let us say that an FCN on Pfizer is close to maturity with a strike of USD 36 while the prevailing price is USD 34. Since we will be selling a Put Option which is already 'in money', there will be an intrinsic value of the Option. In addition, there will also be a time value as the tenure has been extended. This time value makes the preposition feasible for the Issuer and the Investor. Generally, the Issuer will insist on a minimum size of USD 1 million for such a restructuring.

Chapter 5

OPTIONS — A DEEPER DIVE

While covering the basics of Options in Chapter 2, we purposefully avoided going into the mathematical formulas which are used to calculate the price of an Option. While Options on commodities and other products have been around for hundreds of years, the Chicago Board Options Exchange was the first Exchange to launch listed Options on single stocks in 1973. Initially the pricing of Options was a difficult and complex subject. In fact, for the first four years, only Call Options were traded and Put Options were introduced only in 1977. Options on indices like S&P 500 were introduced even later in 1983. Thankfully, Fischer Black and Myron Scholes came up with a theoretical model for pricing Options in 1973. This model was so revolutionary that they were awarded the Nobel Prize. In order to understand how this model calculates the prices of Options, we need to start with an understanding of Log- normal Distribution.

We have seen a normal distribution in Chapter 2. This distribution is symmetrical in the sense that there are equal number of entries on left and right side of the mean, as seen in Figure 5.1.

There are innumerable traits in nature whose values are normally distributed. We can think of examples ranging from the

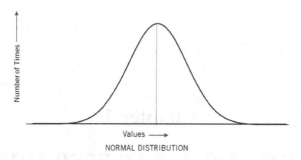

NORMAL DISTRIBUTION

Figure 5.1:   Normal Distribution

height of students in a class to the measurement of Blood Pressure of the residents of a town. The most of residents would have a Blood Pressure of 120/80, there will be some with 130/90 or 110/70, and few with a high reading of 150/110 or 100/50.

In Figure 5.1 above, the values (e.g., 168cm) are on the x-axis and number of times each value occurs is on the y-axis. Let us consider the chart of heights of a class of 30 students. There may be 7 students with a height of 168cm, 5 with 170cm, and 5 with 166cm. The values like 168 cm will appear on the x-axis and the number of times these values occur, e.g., 7 or 5, will be plotted on the y-axis. The values towards the middle occur the greatest number of times and the extreme values occur fewer times. The characteristics of a Normal Distribution include the fact that the Mean, Mode, and Median are all at the same place in the chart. Mean is the average of all values, Mode is the most frequent value, and Median is the midpoint in terms of number of observations. For calculating the Median, we need to arrange all the values in an ascending or descending order and find the value which divides the number of observations equally. So in the graph of the height of 30 students of a class, the number of students on both sides of 168cm will roughly be equal.

As Investors, we are concerned with the question whether stock prices are normally distributed. The Black-Scholes Formula works on the assumption that the stock prices are distributed log normally. So for understanding Black-Scholes, we need to understand Log-normal Distribution.

Let us assume that we invest $10,000 at an annual rate of interest of 10%. If the interest charged is Simple, we will have $11,000 at the end of the year. If the interest is not Simple but Compound, the amount at the end of one year will depend on how frequently the interest is compounded. In the case it is compounded every six months, we will have 11,025. In the case it is compounded every day, we will have $11,051 at the end of one year. The upper limit is reached when the interest is compounded on a continuous basis. Continuous compounding will give us a value of 11,051.7. So the gain with continuous compounding is $1,051.70.

Now let us see what happens when we invest $100,000 in such a way that it loses 10% of its value every year. The value at the end of one year will depend on the frequency at which it loses money. In the case loss is compounded six monthly, we will have $9,025. In the case it is compounded daily, we will have $9,048. Finally, if it is compounded on a continuous basis, we will have $9,048.30 at the end of the year. So, the loss with continuous compounding is $952. We can see that the resultant loss in the case of continuous compounding is lower than the gain with continuous compounding even though the rate of profit and loss was 10% in both cases. This is so because as we increase the frequency of compounding, after each period, we have a relatively higher amount as the base.

Investing in a stock is akin to investing an amount at a rate of interest. Volatility can be viewed as interest rate. Like interest rates, it can be compounded at different intervals. Since stock markets are active throughout the year (barring holidays, of course), it is assumed that the volatility is working on a continuous basis. On some of the days, stock prices move up and on some of the days the stock prices move down. Let us assume that the probability of stock price going up on a particular day is the same as the probability of it going down. Still, due to the compounding effect described above, the positive observations will have higher values as compared to negative values. This will result in a price distribution which will have a smaller number of negative observations and a higher number of positive observations.

In addition, the stock prices cannot go below zero, whereas theoretically there is no bar on how high the prices can go up. So there is a lower bound of zero and unlimited upside. This results in a distribution of prices which are not symmetrical but has a higher number of positive values. This means that the Mean, which is the average value of all observations, will not be in the middle but will be located to the right side. This distribution, which is skewed to the right side, is known as a Log-normal Distribution. Black-Scholes Formula for calculating option prices assumes that stock prices follow a Log-normal Distribution. Graphically, this distribution this distribution is shown in Figure 5.2.

In the lognormal graph above, mode is the value on the x-axis, which has the highest number of observations. Median is the value where the number of observations on each side are equal. Mean is the value on the x-axis where the value of observations on the left and right side are equal (Figure 5.3).

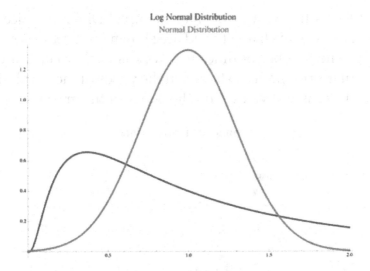

Figure 5.2: Log-normal distribution versus Normal Distribution

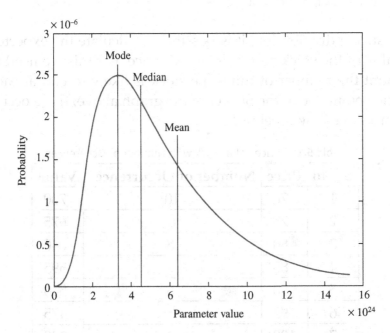

Figure 5.3: Mean, Mode, and Median of a Lognormal Distribution

Now let us try with a concrete example. Different prices at which the stock is likely to end are shown on the x-axis of the graph. The number of times the stock is likely to end at that particular price point is shown on the y-axis of the graph. The Strike Price is shown as X on the x-axis of the graph.

Lognormal Distributions

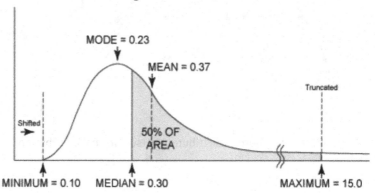

In such a distribution, it is possible to calculate the expected value of the stock above the Strike Price. For this we need to count the number of times the stock is likely to end at each price point above the Strike. In the graph above, these occurrences are shown below.

Table 5.1: Prices of a Stock with Number of Occurences

Sr No	Price	Number of Occurrences	Value
1	70	10	700
2	75	9	675
3	80	8	640
4	85	7	595
5	90	6	540
6	95	5	475
7	100	3	300
Total		48	3925

Let us say that the total number of occurrences is 150, so in 48/150 occurrences, we can be expected to be 'in-the-money'. The average value of stock which will be 'in-the-money' will thus be 3925/150 = 26.16.

As a next step we need to find out the amount that we will have to pay for the exercise of the Call Option. We know that the Strike Price is 70 and the proportion of times that we will be paying this Strike Price is 48/150 = 0.32. So we will be paying 70*0.32 = 22.40 for the exercise of the Option.

Now we know what we will be paying for the exercise and what is the expected value of stock we will receive in lieu of the exercise of this Option. The difference is the value of the Call Option or the expected pay-off from the Call Option.

So essentially, on one hand we estimate the value of Stock that will be above the Strike Price, and on the other hand we estimate the amount that we will be paying for the exercise. The difference between the two values is the value we would be receiving as the Buyer of the Call Option. How much should we be willing to pay for receiving this value in future. For this we need to discount to Present Value by using the interest rate for the period.

The Black-Scholes Formula, while looking complex, is essentially the same. Its first leg determines the total value of stock that will be above the Strike and the second leg estimates the price we will have to pay for the exercise of the Call Option. It is represented as below:

$$C = SN(d_1) - Xe^{-rt}N(d_2)$$

Where

C = Value of Call Option
S = Price of the Stock
X = Exercise Price
e = Exponential Function
r = Annual Interest Rate
t = Time to Expiration

Before proceeding, let us have a look at the expression Xe^{-rt}. This expression is the present value of the Strike Price we will have to pay. We need to calculate the present value because though the Strike Price will have to be paid at a future date, we are trying to ascertain the value of the Call Option and this value is to be paid today. The expression 'e' is the exponential function, which captures the effect of continuous compounding.

Having understood the backbone of Black-Scholes, let us proceed to examine expressions $N(d_1)$ and $N(d_2)$. Expression $N(d_1)$ is the area which represents the proportion of times when the Call Option is 'in-the-money'. This proportion of times is calculated in terms of Standard Deviation. Multiplying this proportion with the Forward Price of the stock gives the average value of all stocks above the exercise price at the time of expiry of the Option. By average we mean the number of occurrences above Strike Price divided by the total number of occurrences. The Formula for calculating the value of d_1 is as below:

$$d_1 = \frac{\ln(S/X) + \{r + (\sigma^2/2)\}t}{\sigma\sqrt{t}}$$

In this equation, In(S/X) is the log of Strike Price to the Stock Price. This is a way of representing the number of times the Strike Price should be raised to get the Stock Price. The second part of the numerator is the adjustment to arrive at the Forward price by multiplying the rate of interest with time. In addition, there is an adjustment relating the Standard Deviation or Volatility. The higher the expected volatility, the higher the value of $\sigma^2 t/2$. Finally, the numerator is divided by one standard deviation ($\sigma\sqrt{t}$) to get the figure of d_1. The purpose of this division is that we wish to know, in terms of Standard Deviation, the distance of the Strike Price from the Forward Price.

This is followed by the calculation of N(d1), which is the average number of times the stock is above the Strike Price. When this is multiplied by the Stock Price, we know that the likely value of the Stock is above the Strike Price. We are not interested in knowing the value of the Stock below Strike, because in that case, the Option will expire and be worthless. We wish to know only the value of the stock that will be above the Strike Price.

Now that we know the average value of the stock, we need to know the amount we will have to pay for the exercise of the Option. We already know the Strike Price. If we know the likelihood of the Option being in the money, we can arrive at the amount we will have to pay for the exercise of Option. The likelihood is nothing but the percentage of number of times the stock price will end up being 'in-the-money'. In any distribution, the Median is the point where the number of occurrences is equal on both sides. In a normal distribution, the Median and Mean are exactly at the same point. However, we are dealing with a Log-normal

Distribution. In this distribution, the right tail is fat and number of occurrences are more to the right side. Hence the Mean is towards right and median is between the Mode and Mean. In other words, the median is to the left of the Mean. How far the Median is to the left of the Mean depends on the volatility of the stock. Since volatility is defined as Standard Deviation, the Median lies to the left of the Mean by a factor of σ.

Let us see the derivation of N(d2). For this we reduce d1 by one standard deviation multiplied by square root of time.

$$D_2 = d_1 - \sigma\sqrt{t}$$

Now $N(d_2)$ is the cumulative probability of the Option ending up 'in-the-money'. This means that it takes into account all the occurrences when the Stock Price will end such that the holder of the Call Option will be able to exercise this. When we multiply $N(d_2)$ by the Strike Price, we get the amount the holder of the Call Option will have to pay for the exercise of the Option.

While the first expression in the Black-Sholes formula helps us arrive at the value of stock that will be 'in-the-money', the second expression helps us find out the amount required to be paid for the exercise of the Call Option. The difference of the two is the theoretical price of the Call Option.

PUT-CALL PARITY

Once we know the theoretical price of a Call Option, deriving the price of the Put Option of same maturity and same Strike is not difficult. The relationship between the price of a Call Option and a Put Option is given by the following formula:

$$C + X = P + F$$

where:

C = Price of Call Option
P = Price of Put Option
X = Strike Price
F = Future Price

Let us say a stock is trading at $100 and the Forward is priced at $102. A call of Strike $95 is available for a price of $9. Going by this formula, the price of the Put has to be $2. In other words, $9 + $95 = $2 + $102 has to hold true. If this formula does not hold, there will be arbitrage opportunities.

Chapter 6

PERSPECTIVE OF THE ISSUER

So far we have been looking at various aspects from the perspective of an Investor. One usual curiosity in the mind of an Investor is that if Fixed Coupon Notes (FCNs) are such good products, and if I stand to earn decent money, someone must be losing money. Or the Investor may wonder what the actual science behind these products is.

As FCNs grew in popularity, the Issuers have refined the formulas to price these. Based on the input values, these formulas are able to provide a price for FCNs in a matter of minutes if not seconds. The process flow is depicted in Figure 6.1.

Inputs like underlying stocks, duration, Strike, and autocallability are provided by the Wealth Manager while approaching the Issuer for a quote. The Issuer already has a view on interest rates, which does not change so frequently. However, they need to have the value of Implied Volatility and also the Implied Correlation between the underlying stocks. Now the Implied Volatility for the stocks which have listed Options can be determined by backward calculation from the Option price. For the stocks which do not have listed Options, the Issuers have various formulas. For example, they may derive the Implied Volatility of a stock based on another similar

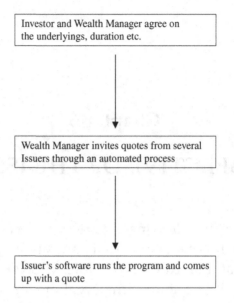

Figure 6.1: Process Flow for Initiation of an FCN

stock or based on the Implied Volatility of the Index. Similarly, the Issuer has to take a view on the Implied Correlation of the stocks requested. They may and may not give weightage to historical correlation between these stocks.

The differences in opinion about future expected volatility and the future expected correlation between the stocks is what leads to different prices for the same Product from different Issuers. Different Issuers may have different risk appetites at different points of time. It may happen that we are towards the fag end of the year and one Issuer has not reached the targets for the year and is more keen to attract business. Or it could be that the Issuer has incurred some losses in some other part of the business and wishes to take minimum risk. Naturally, he will quote a lower price. There could be an Issuer who has recently entered this business and needs to establish himself as a credible player in the market. Or the Credit Risk rating of an Issuer is due for review and the rating agency views the risk more conservatively.

Having taken a view on the future expected volatility and future expected correlation, do the Issuers price the option using the Black-Scholes Formula? No, the formula does not provide a solution for Options which have more than one underlying and has to take correlation into consideration. For FCNs, almost invariably the Issuer will use the Monte Carlo Simulation to project where the sock prices are likely to end.

MONTE CARLO SIMULATION

While Vanilla Options can be priced using the Black-Scholes Formula with a reasonable degree of accuracy, this Formula is not of much help in pricing Exotic Options. When we consider FCNs, usually we need to price a Put Option on the worst of three stocks. For pricing such Options, the Issuers have to use mathematical models which have Monte Carlo processes as their backbone. When a Wealth Manager approaches an Issuer to provide a quote for an FCN, the trader will input various values in these mathematical models. Besides the usual inputs like Stock Price, Strike, Duration, Interest Rate, Implied Volatility, etc., these inputs will include the Implied Correlation between the underlyings. Based on these inputs, the Monte Carlo process will run thousands of iterations as to the possible values of the underlyings at the end of the period.

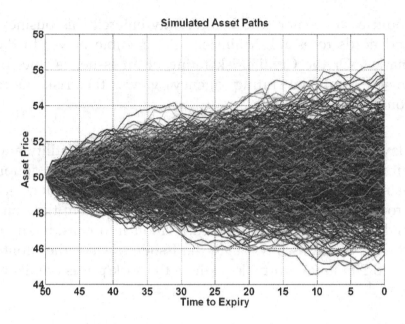

Figure 6.2: Monte Carlo Simulation

These iterations will be run as per the parameters decided by the Investor and his Wealth Manager. This is what is called the Generator function of the Monte Carlo function. For example, in the case of the price of a Bond at some distance in time, we need to multiply the Principal with the rate of interest and time, as shown below:

$$B_t = B_0 *r*t$$

Where B_0 is the initial price of Bond, r is the rate of interest, and t is the time lapsed. Of course, the assumption is that the interest rates have not moved. This formula constitutes the Generator function for Bonds. While the price is expected to appreciate with time at the rate of interest in the case of Bonds, the situation is more complex in the case of Stock Prices. The Equity prices are likely to appreciate by a

Risk-Free rate of interest plus a Risk Premium. The Risk Premium can be viewed as additional compensation demanded by the Investors for holding Equities which are volatile as compared to the stable returns from investing in Bonds. So if we have to devise a formula for estimating the stock prices at a given point of time, we need to consider both the Risk Free rate of return as well as the volatility.

The software for generating these values is pretty much standardized across different Issuers. In fact, globally there are only two or three providers of this software. This software is quite sophisticated and even the traders working with these Issuers may not know the intricacies of the formulas. Still it is not difficult to understand the logic behind this software. In fact, Microsoft Excel has an in-built Monte Carlo model. It starts by generating a random number through the function RAND(). This function gives a random number

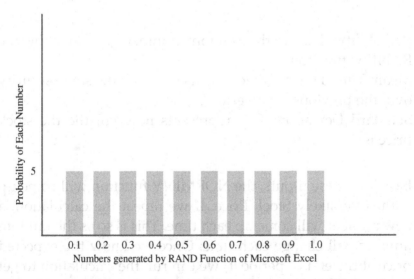

Figure 6.3: Probability of Different Numbers Generated by RAND Function of Microsoft Excel

between 0 and 1. Excel throws these numbers such that these are uniformly distributed, i.e., the probability of occurrence of each number is equal.

However, we know that in real life, the probability of different stock prices is not equal. So this random number needs to be modified to account for the standard distribution of stock prices. This random number is then converted into a value Z_t, which is the distance of this random number from the Mean in terms of Standard Deviation. This is achieved by the = NORMSINV function in Excel. Z_t is next multiplied by Volatility times the Square root of time to give the random piece of a Stock Price. This can be combined with the fixed piece to get the likely Stock Price at the end of period 1.

Another Excel function is NORMINV, which gives the likely price based on average returns in the past and Standard Deviation. This function requires the following inputs:

Probability: This is the random number generated by the RAND () function
Mean: This is the average returns given by the same security over the previous time period
Standard Deviation: This represents how volatile the stock price is

Based on these inputs, the NORMINV function will come up with some likely Stock Price. If we repeat the calculation, a new number will come up each time. This is so as the random number will change each time. Once we know the expected price at the end of period 1, we can run the calculation to get the expected price at the end of period 2, and so on. Continuing like this, we can get the price at the end of our desired period.

When we run these iterations several times, the end result will be different each time. Each result will represent one likely price at the end of the period. While none of these prices may be correct, the average of these prices will be close to being correct.

Since we can define the Generator function whichever way we like, it is possible to price Exotic Options like the Worst of Put, which are the basis of pricing FCNs.

RISK MANAGEMENT OF THE ISSUER

Once the Issuer has given a quote, which has been accepted by the Wealth Manager on behalf of the client, the Issuer will try to hedge the Risk to the maximum extent possible. We have seen that the Investor in the FCN is Short Put Option on the underlying stocks and the Issuer is Long the Put Option. The Risks associated with Option trades are best described using Greek notations or simply Greeks.

DELTA

This is the most important Greek. Let us take the example of a Call Option which is deep 'in-the-money'. The price of this Call Option comprises mainly the embedded value or difference between the Forward Price of the stock and the Strike. The price of the Call Option, which is deep 'in-the-money', moves almost in tandem with the movement of the price of the underlying. As against this, a Call Option which is 'at-the-money' (Forward Price being equal to the Strike Price) will not move in tandem. A 1% rise in the Stock Price may lead to only a 0.5% rise in the price of the Call Option. This ratio of change in the price of the Option to the change in the price of the underlying is known as Delta.

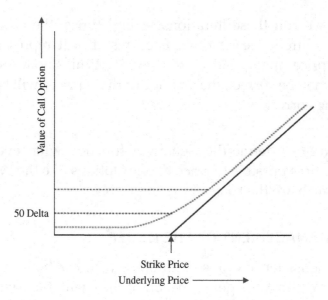

Figure 6.4:   Delta of a Call Option

$$\text{Delta} = \frac{\Delta \, \text{change in the value of option}}{\Delta \, \text{change in the value of underlying}}$$

Call Options have the Delta values ranging from 0 to 100. A value of zero means that the option is deep 'out-of-the-money' and a small increase in the price of the underlying will not have any effect on the price of the Call Option.

As against this, the value of a Put Option decreases with the increase in the price of the underlying. So Put Options have negative values ranging from –100 to 0. A deep 'in-the-money' Put Option will have a delta of –100, which means that a 1% decrease in the price of the underlying will increase the value of the Put Option by 1% (Figure 6.5).

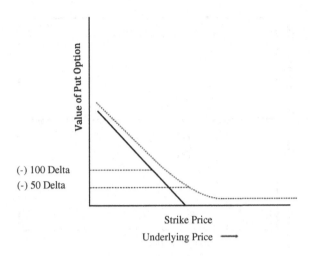

Figure 6.5: Delta of Put Option

Delta can also be viewed as the probability of the Option ending up being 'in-the-money'. A Delta of 50 means that there is a 50% probability of the Call Option ending up being 'in-the-money'. We will shortly return to the concept of Delta as it is the most important Greek in hedging the Risk of an open Option position.

GAMMA

As the price of the underlying stock changes, even the value of Delta also changes. When the values of Delta are closer to 50 or –50, a 1% change in the price of the underlying may lead to a 1% change in the value of Delta. However, as the value of Delta moves towards 100 or –100, the pace of change of Delta goes down. When we represent this on a graph (Figure 6.6), the slope of the line can be seen as becoming flatter.

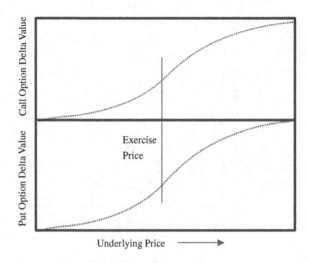

Figure 6.6:   Gamma of Call and Put Options

THETA

Theta is nothing but the time value of an Option. As we approach the expiry date, the price of the Option will come closer to the price of the underlying. This can be seen in Figures 6.7 and 6.8 below.

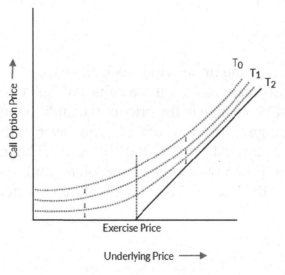

Figure 6.7:   Theta of a Call Option

Figure 6.8: Theta of a Put Option

VEGA

The price of an Option is also sensitive to the volatility of the underlying equity. As the volatility increases, the prices of both the Call and Put Options increase. And as the volatility decreases, the prices of both Call and Put Options decrease. This has an implication for the price of an FCN in the secondary market. Let us say that an Investor has invested in a one-year FCN and six months have already lapsed. The Investor wishes to wind up his position and approaches the Issuer for the same. The Issuer will simply reprice the FCN as a new trade and the prevailing volatility will have the effect on the pricing of the FCN.

RHO

Rho is the sensitivity of the price of an Option to the change in interest rates. Since interest rates are the least important factor in determining the price of an Option, Rho does not

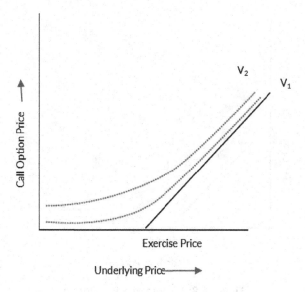

Figure 6.9:   Vega of a Call Option

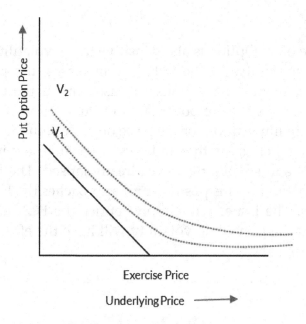

Figure 6.10:   Vega of a Put Option

play a significant role in Risk Management of existing Option position.

DYNAMIC HEDGING

When an Issuer issues an FCN, it is a Long Put Option on the underlying and is also Long on the correlation between the underlyings. The initial Delta position of the Issuer is negative. However, the Issuer wishes to maintain a neutral position of Delta. So the Issuer will buy the underlying shares on Day 0 to bring the overall position to zero. Till such time the Issuer has been able to buy the required shares in the market, the Issuer will not issue the trade confirmation. The Issuer will like to buy the underlying shares without moving the market, thus will like to limit the buying to a certain percentage of the turnover of that particular stock in the market. This is also the reason why FCNs can be done only on Equities which are fairly liquid. Sometimes, the Issuer may have a prescribed limit for a particular stock on a particular day. The Issuer will not enter into a trade beyond a size which can be hedged in the market. This hedging can also be viewed from the perspective as to what will happen on maturity.

Being Long on the Put Option, on maturity, the Issuer may like to exercise his Put Option. Of course, he will do so only if the underlying Stock Price is below the Strike Price. Since the FCNs on Equities are generally not Cash Settled, the Issuer may be required to deliver the shares. On day 0, the Issuer will buy a certain number of shares and later on will keep changing the number of these shares depending on the change in the value of Delta. Most of the Issuers will be carrying out this exercise at the start of each working day. When done systematically over a long period and over a large number of trades, the mathematical models (Black-Scholes or Monte Carlo) hold true.

So the position of the Issuer is akin to that of a casino operator, who offers the odds such that the probability of the operator winning over a large number of bets is almost a certainty.

Chapter 7

VARIANTS OF FIXED COUPON NOTES (FCNS)

EQUITY LINKED NOTE

An Equity Linked Note (ELN) is a Structured Product, which is similar to an FCN in the sense that both have a Sale of Put Option at their core feature. While an FCN usually has more than one underlying, an ELN is usually on one single underlying Equity or Equity Index.

Another difference is that the tenure of an ELN is usually 30 days and it is rare to see a tenure of more than three months. As against this, an FCN is usually 6 months or more in duration.

Given the short tenure, there is usually no Coupon paid for an ELN. Instead, an ELN is issued at a discount to the Face Value. At maturity, the Investor gets back the Face Value. The difference between the Issue Price and the Face Value is the income.

Let us say that we do a one-month FCN on Apple Inc. with a Strike Price of USD 300 when it is trading at USD 320. Let us say that the ELN was issued at a price of USD 99 and the tenure was one month. Since the Investor is earning USD 1 over a period of one month, annualized yield works out to be 12.12% p.a. At the end of one month, in case the stock is trading above USD 300, the Investor gets back USD 100. In case the stock is trading below USD 300, the Investor will be delivered the stock at a price of USD 300 per share.

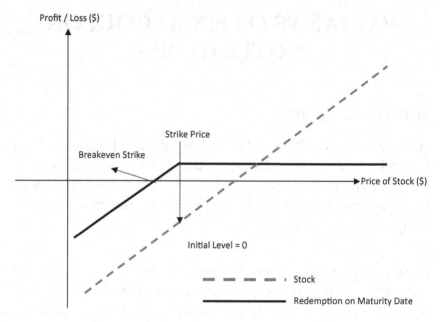

Figure 7.1:   Pay Off Digram of an Equity Linked Note

REVERSE CONVERTIBLE

Reverse Convertibles (RCs) are nothing but FCNs with a different name. RCs are more popular in Europe and FCNs are more popular in Asia. Sometimes, RCs are structured in such a manner that Strike is 100, i.e., the Strike is the same as the initial level. Such RCs have a Knock-In feature, which means that the Strike becomes relevant only if the Knock-In barrier was breached. Since the Investor is taking a higher Risk by agreeing to a higher Strike, usually the Knock-In is lower than the Strike of an FCN with comparable features. The Knock-In can be European or American. In the case of a European Knock In, what matters is the final observation. In case the price of the worst performing share is below the Knock-In level on final observation, the Note is supposed to have Knocked-In. In such a scenario, the Investor will get the delivery of the worst performing share at Strike Price.

Let us try to understand with the following example:

Duration: 1 Year
Strike Price: 100%
Coupon: 8% p.a.
European Knock-In: 65%
Coupon Frequency: Quarterly
Underlyings: Apple, Johnson & Johnson, Amazon

Scenario 1: The worst underlying closes above Knock-In. In such a case, the Note has not Knocked-In and the Principal is redeemed with Coupon.

Scenario 2: Let us say that the worst performing share closes below Knock-In level. In such a case, the Investor is delivered the worst performing stock at a price of 100. Since the stock is trading below 65, the losses are substantial.

In case the Knock-In feature is American, then what matters is the daily closing price. In case any one of the underlyings breaches the Knock-In level on any of the daily closings, the Note will be supposed to have knocked-in. However, the Note will continue till maturity and the final

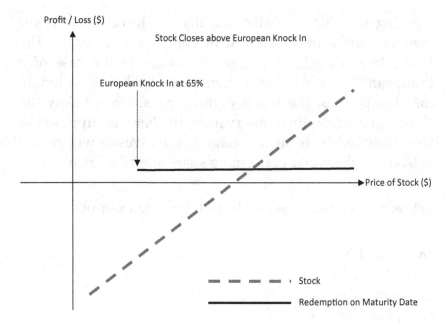

Figure 7.2:   Pay off Diagram When Stock Closes Above European Knock In

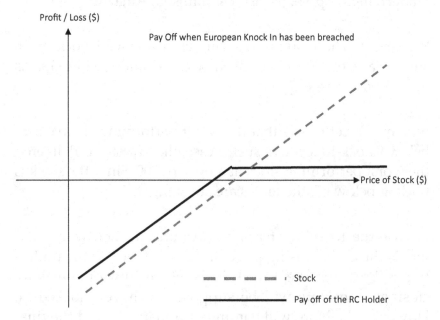

Figure 7.3:   Pay off Diagram When Stock Closes Below European Knock In

Risk Reward will depend on the final closing price of the worst underlying. Unlike the two scenarios above, here we could have a third scenario. It is possible that the worst performing stock breaches the Knock-In level during the life of the Note. So the Note has Knocked-In. However, on the Final Observation Date, all the underlyings close above Strike. In such a case, the Investor will get his Principal and Coupon back.

PHOENIX NOTE WITH MEMORY COUPON

In this variation, the Coupon is also subject to a certain condition. For example, the quarterly Coupon will be paid only if the worst performing stock closes above the Coupon barrier. Let us say we have a Note with the following features:

Duration: 2 Years
Strike Price: 100%
Coupon: 8% p.a.
Coupon Frequency: Quarterly
Coupon Barrie: 65%
Memory Coupon: Applicable

In such a Note, there is an observation at the end of each quarter. In case all the underlyings close above the Coupon Barrier, the Issuer pays a coupon of 2% and the Note continues to the next quarter. In case one or more of the underlyings close below the Coupon Barrier, no Coupon is paid. At the end of the next quarter, in case all the underlyings close above the Coupon Barrier, the Coupon is paid for the current quarter as well as the previous quarter. Thus the Note is said to have Memory. Since from the perspective of the Coupon payment the Note was dead, and has now revived, it is akin to a Phoenix which rises from the ashes, hence the name Phoenix.

ATHENA

Athena is another Note where the Coupon is quite high as compared to a normal FCN. This is achieved by subjecting the Coupon to a Barrier of 100%. This means that on each observation date, the Coupon will be paid only if the underlying is above the initial level.

There is an Autocall feature as well. In case the underlying closes above the Autocall level, the Product is autocalled. In case the Coupon Barrier and the Autocall level are both at 100%, and underlying closes above 100%, the Product is autocalled and the Coupon for the period is paid. If it is below 100%, the Product continues.

On Maturity, if the underlying closes above the Strike, the Investor gets his Principal back. Otherwise he gets the shares at Strike Price.

DAILY RANGE ACCRUAL NOTE

In these Notes, the Coupon is conditional. There is a daily observation and in case all the underlyings close above the Strike, the Coupon gets accrued. On the days when any of the underlying closes below the Strike, there is no Coupon. Of course, the accrued Coupon will be paid once a quarter. Since the Investor is taking the risk of not receiving any Coupon on a certain number of days, he is awarded in the form of lower Strike or higher rate of Coupon.

FCNS ON UNDERLYINGS OTHER THAN EQUITIES

Though most of the discussion in this book is based on Equities, it is by no means the whole universe. Actually, it is possible to do FCNs where the underlyings are not Equities. Any asset which is liquid and has volatility can be an under- lying for an FCN. One possible way of finding such assets is the Volatility and Correlation Analysis (VCA) function of Bloomberg. In this function, we can see the Historical and Implied Volatilities of various assets.

Reproduced below is the screenshot of the page show- ing volatilities of Real Estate exchange-traded funds (ETFs).

		Vol	Chg	Low	Range	1M 100% Implied Volatility				
Underlying						High	Avg	+/-	PCTL StdDev	#SD
120)Direxion Daily Real Estate Be		34.65	-1.10	30.04		39.34	34.05	.60	47.73 2.65	.23
121)Direxion Daily Real Estate Bu		32.76	-2.21	29.08		37.65	33.24	-.48	38.64 2.52	-.19
122)Invesco China Real Estate ETF		54.86	.01	13.96		58.85	48.84	6.03	75.00 9.76	.62
123)NEXT FUNDS REIT INDEX ETF		8.47	.71	4.35		8.47	7.21	1.26	93.48 .82	1.52
124)ProShares Ultra Real Estate		23.22	.39	19.51		27.63	22.92	.30	52.27 2.22	.14
125)ProShares UltraShort Real Est		24.10	.13	20.72		29.31	24.00	.11	52.27 2.23	.05
126)Vanguard Real Estate ETF		10.52	.83	9.04		13.26	10.96	.44	38.64 1.15	-.38
127)iShares Cohen & Steers REIT E		12.54	-1.23	9.74		17.18	12.65	-.11	56.82 2.07	-.05
128)iShares S&P/TSX Capped REIT I		11.58	.82	9.05		12.68	11.10	.48	52.27 1.12	.43
129)iShares U.S. Real Estate ETF		10.28	.75	9.00		12.55	10.61	-.33	38.64 .97	-.34

Figure 7.4:   Volatilities of Real Estate ETFs

Next we can see some examples of Bond ETFs.

Underlying	Vol	Chg	Low	Range	High	Avg	+/-	PCTL	StdDev	#SD
Direxion Daily 20 Year Plus T	36.39	-1.63	33.15		39.24	35.69	.70	61.36	1.78	.40
Direxion Daily 20 Year Plus T	37.00	.67	32.99		39.18	35.80	1.20	61.36	1.89	.63
Direxion Daily 7-10 Year Trea	21.01	4.33	15.52		39.21	19.42	1.59	72.50	6.03	.26
Invesco Emerging Markets Sove	6.22	.50	4.89		15.37	7.96	-1.74	43.18	3.22	-.54
ProShares Short 20+ Year Trea	11.92	-.21	10.45		15.58	12.27	-.35	29.55	1.01	-.35
ProShares Short High Yield	13.00	5.63	7.11		13.95	11.20	1.79	79.55	2.00	.89
ProShares Ultra 20+ Year Trea	24.00	-.91	21.27		25.28	23.29	.71	61.36	1.14	.62
ProShares Ultra 7-10 Year Tre	11.15	.13	10.31		11.62	10.85	.30	57.50	.40	.77
ProShares UltraShort 20+ Year	23.25	-.38	20.93		25.80	23.24	.01	52.27	1.40	.01
ProShares UltraShort Lehman 7	11.05	.28	9.72		12.66	10.83	.23	65.91	.74	.31
SPDR Bloomberg Barclays High	4.75	-.39	3.61		5.14	4.15	.59	84.09	.35	1.70
SPDR Bloomberg Barclays Inter	7.35	-.68	7.08		9.15	7.83	-.40	15.91	.50	-.96
Vanguard Total Bond Market ET	4.20	-.10	3.67		4.36	4.03	.18	70.45	.18	.97
iShares 1-3 Year Treasury Bon	2.19	.28	1.66		4.00	2.08	.11	75.00	.52	.21
iShares 20+ Year Treasury Bon	11.68	-.49	10.71		12.92	11.74	-.07	52.27	.62	-.11
iShares 3-7 Year Treasury Bon	3.12	-.04	2.75		6.77	3.82	-.70	29.55	1.16	-.60
iShares 7-10 Year Treasury Bo	5.32	-.28	4.68		12.79	5.97	-.64	20.45	1.62	-.40
iShares Core U.S. Aggregate B	4.43	-.22	4.00		4.65	4.31	.13	65.91	.19	.65
iShares JP Morgan USD Emergin	5.57	-.54	4.87		6.23	5.56	.01	43.18	.44	.02
iShares National Muni Bond ET	2.94	-.03	2.53		4.29	2.98	-.04	61.36	.46	-.08
iShares TIPS Bond ETF	4.85	.14	4.69		5.39	4.96	-.11	38.64	.20	-.53

Figure 7.5: Volatilities of Bond ETFs

And finally some examples of Commodity ETFs.

Underlying	Vol	Chg	Low	Range	High	Avg	+/-	PCTL	StdDev	#SD
Aberdeen Standard Physical Go	10.58	.13	9.06		52.92	20.65	-10.07	27.50	15.01	-.67
Aberdeen Standard Physical Si	16.94	-1.73	15.03		22.63	18.40	-1.45	20.45	1.80	-.81
BetaPro Crude Oil 2x Daily Bu	59.33	5.36	48.41		76.58	58.52	2.81	67.39	6.61	.42
BetaPro Natural Gas -2x Daily	85.08	-5.86	72.90		101.06	85.06	.02	58.70	6.42	.00
BetaPro Natural Gas 2x Daily	69.19	25.64	69.19		100.20	86.06	-16.87	.00	7.84	-2.15
Direxion Daily Energy Bear 3X	61.99	-1.84	52.37		63.84	56.77	5.22	88.64	2.59	2.01
Direxion Daily Energy Bull 3X	56.43	.02	52.51		58.00	55.43	1.00	56.82	1.53	.65
Direxion Daily Natural Gas Re	101.00	-6.72	93.15		107.72	99.70	1.29	61.36	3.74	.35
Invesco DB Agriculture Fund	11.90	.31	9.57		15.12	11.88	.02	43.18	1.05	.02
Invesco DB Base Metals Fund	30.80	.15	25.54		57.89	33.76	-2.97	56.82	8.47	-.35
Invesco DB Commodity Index Tr	14.34	-2.26	14.34		17.72	16.20	-1.86	.00	.91	-2.05
Invesco DB Energy Fund	38.19	9.92	21.80		46.90	30.39	7.80	69.05	9.16	.85
Invesco DB Gold Fund	17.68	2.94	11.55		18.64	16.09	1.59	64.29	2.15	.74
Invesco DB Oil Fund	28.83	.56	26.35		51.66	29.17	-.34	61.36	5.03	-.07
Invesco DB Precious Metals Fu	18.69	-1.41	15.37		21.73	18.52	.18	38.24	2.11	.08
Invesco DB Silver Fund	16.62	.90	16.62		24.19	19.81	-3.20	.00	2.95	-1.08
ProShares Ultra Basic Materia	30.59	-3.90	23.74		74.69	33.77	-3.18	61.36	13.33	-.24
ProShares Ultra Bloomberg Cru	59.62	-2.66	56.24		64.88	60.65	-1.03	29.55	2.50	-.41
ProShares Ultra Bloomberg Nat	109.30	-.99	96.49		110.29	103.89	5.41	84.09	3.59	1.51
ProShares Ultra Gold	20.55	-1.31	18.67		32.09	21.82	-1.27	43.18	3.39	-.38
ProShares Ultra Silver	33.40	-1.48	31.08		43.13	36.13	-2.73	20.45	3.31	-.82

Figure 7.6: Volatilities of Commodity ETFs

FCN ON LIBOR

There are times when the Implied Volatility on the London Inter-bank Offered Rate (LIBOR) goes very high. Typically these are the times when the Central Banks start reducing the benchmark rates. The rationale for FCN is that it can be used as a hedging tool. Many Investors have borrowings either against their portfolios, or have mortgages or borrowings in their corporate entities. Many of these borrowings are at a floating rate with a base rate tied to LIBOR. The Risk in this FCN is that the Investor will suffer in case LIBOR goes down significantly. In such a scenario, the cost of borrowing will go down and the Investor will gain on that side. In case LIBOR goes down but does not go down below Strike, the Investor will benefit from both sides. On one hand he will be earning a Coupon on interest and on the other hand his cost of borrowing would have gone down. An example of such an FCN is reproduced below.

Issuer	SG Issuer (SGIS), Luxembourg	Tenor	12 Months
Rating	Guaranteed by Société Générale (A1/A/A) - (Moody's / S&P / Fitch)	Issue Price	100%
Specified Currency	USD	Denomination	50,000 USD
Initial Valuation Date	24 June 2019	Final Valuation Date	30 June 2020
Issue Date	08 July 2019	Maturity Date	08 July 2020
Strike Price	38.30% of the initial price	ISIN	XS1994893649
Coupon Amount	8% p.a.	Settlement Type	Physical Settlement
Autocall Level	100%	Autocall Frequency	Non Call 3 Months, Monthly Call thereafter
Coupon Frequency	Monthly		

Issuer

SG Issuer (SGIS), Luxembourg

Guaranteed by Société Générale (A1/A/A) - (Moody's / S&P / Fitch)

The investor is bearing the credit risk of the Note's Issuer.

Underlying Description

Name	Bloomberg Ticker	Initial Price	Autocall Level	Strike Price
3 months USD LIBOR	US0003M Index	2.3492%	2.3492%	0.8997%

Figure 7.7: Terms of an FCN of US LIBOR

Chapter 8

IMPACT OF COVID 19 TURMOIL ON FIXED COUPON NOTES (FCNS)

Let us see the journey of an FCN through the turmoil of the COVID-19 Pandemic. A 12-month FCN on the worst of Alexion Pharmaceuticals, Bank of America, and Facebook was done on June 12, 2019 with a Strike of 64.03% and Coupon of 8%. The FCN was autocallable on a quarterly basis if all three underlyings closed above initial level on any of the observation dates. The initial levels were as follows.

Table 8.1: Initial Terms of an FCN

Name	Initial Spot	Autocall Level	Strike Price
Alexion Pharmaceuticals	117.11	117.11	74.98
Bank of America	28.17	28.17	18.03
Facebook	178.65	178.65	114.38

The prices of the underlyings on the first, second, and third observation dates were as follows:

Table 8.2: Prices of Underlyings on Observation Dates

Name	Autocall Level	First Observation Date September 30, 2019	Second Observation Date December 27, 2019	Third Observation Date March 30, 2020
Alexion Pharmaceuticals	117.11	97.74	108.55	87.26
Bank of America	28.17	29.17	35.35	22.04
Facebook	178.65	178.08	208.10	165.95
Comments		Alexion Pharma and Facebook are below Autocall level. So the Coupon for the first quarter is paid and the Product continues	Alexion Pharma is below Autocall level. So the Coupon for the second quarter is paid and the Product continues	All three underlyings are below Autocall Level. So the Coupon for the third quarter is paid and the Product continues to Maturity.

So the Product was not autocalled on the first, second, or third observation dates. On the Final Observation Date, the autocall level does not matter. Only material thing is whether any of the underlyings closed below the Strike Price. If more than one underlying closed below the Strike Price, the Investor will get the delivery of the worst performing underlying. In case all three underlyings close above their respective Strike Levels, the Investor will get his Principal back. Coupon is paid in both situations.

Though the Product is continuing to maturity, the Mark-to-Market price of the Product will keep on varying depending on the prices of the underlyings. The prices were as follows:

Table 8.3:   Prices of FCN and the Underlyings on Different Dates

	September 30, 2019	December 27, 2019	February 20, 2020	March 24, 2020	March 30, 2020
FCN	98.30	102.01	101.57	88.06	90.88
Alexion Pharmaceuticals	97.74	108.55	102.51	85.90	87.26
Bank of America	29.17	35.35	34.85	21.02	22.04
Facebook	178.08	208.10	214.58	161.21	165.95

The S&P 500 Index was at an all-time high on February 19, 2020 and had crashed to its lowest level on March 23, 2020. Since the prices of an FCN depend on closing prices, the true effect of the changes in the prices of the underlying get reflected in the price of the FCN the next day. The price of this particular FCN on February 20, 2020 was 101.57. This price reflects two facts. First being that all three underlyings are above their respective Strike Prices on February 20. Second being that given the low Implied Volatility on that day, the Issuer expects the underlyings to close above their respective Strike Prices on Maturity Date. The price of an FCN will generally not go above 102 because the maximum liability of the Issuer is the Principal and the Coupon. Technically, the maximum liability of the Issuer on the date of Issue was the Principal plurs 8%, but the Issuer will generally be willing to buy back the Note by paying the Coupon for one quarter only.

Also noteworthy is the price of the FCN on March 24, 2020. This was the depth of markets due to the COVID-19 scare. Still all three underlyings were trading above their respective Strike Prices and the Issuer had given a Mark-to-Market price of 88.06. It is normal for an Investor to wonder why the Issuer is pricing the FCN at such a low price when the underlyings are above their Strike. When thinking like this, the Investor is thinking of intrinsic value. The Investor is Short a Put Option

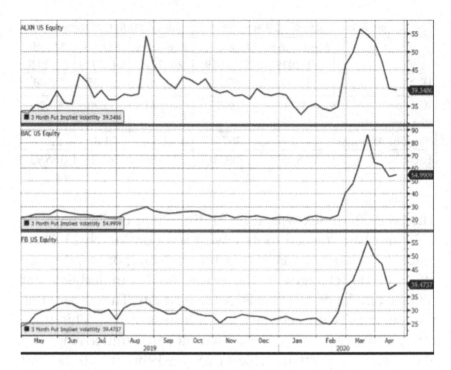

Figure 8.1: Implied Volatilities of Three Underlyings

on the underlying stocks. The value of a Put Option comprises of two components: intrinsic value and time value. While the Buyer of a Put Option (Issuer) is not having intrinsic value in his favor, time value is still in his favor. Another way to look at the situation is from the angle of Implied Volatility. In times of such extraordinary stress, the Implied Volatility of markets, as reflected in the VIX index, shoots through the roof. Implied Volatility of individual stocks is even higher.

Due to this higher Implied Volatility, the price of the Put Option goes up significantly. This higher price of the Put Option, which has already been sold by the Investor, is reflected in the lower Mark-to-Market price of the FCN. We can see from the Chart of Implied Volatility of the three underlying stocks that these were highest around March 23. This led to a spike in the price of Put Options and hence a fall in the price of the FCN. Another way to look at the effect of higher Implied Volatility is through the prism of Probability. The higher the Implied Volatility, the higher the chances that one or more underlyings will end up below their Strike on the Final Observation Date. Whichever way we look at it, the Investor cannot look at merely the intrinsic value and needs to consider the time value as well.

There is one more factor which should affect the price of the FCN. The Investor in an FCN is long correlation and short dispersion of the underlying stocks. The Issuer of the the FCN has a desire for higher dispersion because higher dispersion increases the chances of at least one stock closing below the Strike Price. In times of stress like the COVID-19 pandemic, correlation goes up. This has the effect of not reducing the price of the FCN as much as it would have if there was only one stock involved. This is reflected in the Charts of Correlation below.

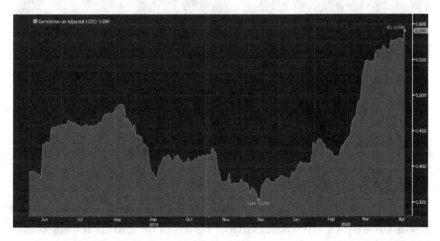

Figure 8.2:   Correlation of Price Movements of Alexion and Facebook

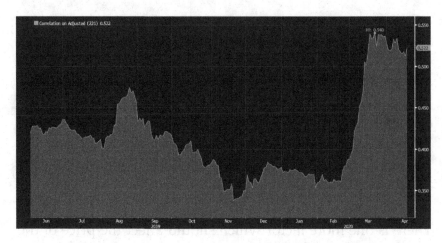

Figure 8.3:   Correlation of Price Movements of Alexion and Bank of America

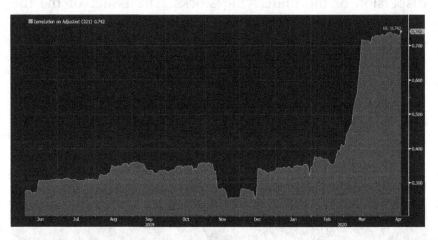

Figure 8.4:   Correlation of Price Movements of Bank of America and Facebook

Let us look at one more example of the change in price of an FCN. A 12-month FCN on the worst of Amazon, Citigroup, and Comcast was done on December 27, 2019 with a Strike of 76.38% and Coupon of 8%. The FCN was autocallable on a quarterly basis if all three underlyings closed above initial level on any of the observation dates. The initial levels were as follows.

Name	Initial Spot	Autocall Level	Strike Price
Amazon	1882.92	1882.92	1438.17
Citigroup	80	80	61.10
Comcast	45.09	45.09	34.43

The price of the FCN as on March 23, 2020 was 67.45. There is an important implication of Mark-to-Market Price. This comes into play if the Investor has taken leverage against his position. Most of the Wealth Managers provide leverage of the same level as the underlying. Let us say that the Lending Value on Facebook, Alexion, and Bank of America is 70%. The FCN with these underlyings will have 70% leverage. As the price of the FCN comes down, the Investor will face a Margin Call. Inability to cover the shortfall would mean that the Investor's position will be liquidated. If the Investor is able to meet the shortfall from some other source, the position is continued and there is a possibility that the price of the FCN will recover. So leverage enhances the return both on the upside as well as on the downside.

Printed in the United States
by Baker & Taylor Publisher Services